FinTech and Data Privacy in Germany

D1807132

Gregor Dorfleitner • Lars Hornuf

FinTech and Data Privacy in Germany

An Empirical Analysis with Policy
Recommendations

 Springer

Gregor Dorfleitner
Center of Finance
University of Regensburg
Regensburg, Germany

Lars Hornuf
Faculty of Business Studies and Economics
University of Bremen
Bremen, Germany

ISBN 978-3-030-31337-1   ISBN 978-3-030-31335-7   (eBook)
https://doi.org/10.1007/978-3-030-31335-7

Translation from the German language edition: FinTech und Datenschutz by Gregor Dorfleitner and Lars Hornuf Copyright © Springer Fachmedien Wiesbaden GmbH, ein Teil von Springer Nature 2019. All Rights Reserved.

This Springer imprint is published by the registered company Springer Nature Switzerland AG.
The registered company address is: Gewerbestrasse 11, 6330 Cham, Switzerland

Foreword

FinTech has become one of the keywords associated with the digitalization of the financial sector and the data-driven economy more generally. In contrast, data protection was certainly a legal keyword in 2018, the year the General Data Protection Regulation ("GDPR") became binding. It follows that research at the intersection of FinTech services and data protection law promises to be particularly exciting due to a large number of unanswered questions regarding their interaction. This book provides an important first step in examining related issues from an empirical perspective.

The book provides the reader with an empirical overview of the substance of the data protection policies of numerous FinTech companies. Despite the fact that financial data as such is not to be regarded as sensitive data under the GDPR, such data nevertheless reveals a lot of important, and oftentimes indeed sensitive, information about users. It is often only through access to financial data that a company receives information about our preferences, habits, or location. This makes this type of data particularly sought-after but also in need of protection. After an introductory presentation of FinTech players in Germany, the authors turn to consider how FinTech companies have implemented their data protection policies. To this end, the data protection statements of more than 500 FinTech companies are analyzed down to the smallest detail. While the third chapter concentrates on the time period from October to December 2017, Chap. 4 deals with the short period after the GDPR became binding. The book closes with an overview of the numerous FinTech business models and questions regarding the regulatory needs of the German FinTech market.

What is particularly noteworthy about this book is the speed with which the two authors have carried out their research. Empirical research on data protection is of immense importance. For example, it gives us answers to questions such as how legislation has been implemented in practice and whether legislative requirements are being followed properly by their respective addressees. Furthermore, the concrete effects of data protection on the data-driven economy become apparent. This is particularly relevant when evaluating whether the GDPR has achieved its desired effects. Of course, there were still some uncertainties about the implementation of the GDPR during the period that is analyzed in this book. This feeling of uncertainty did not only affect FinTech companies but was also evident across all sectors. For instance, a study carried out by the German digital association Bitkom (2018) underlined that even four months after the GDPR became binding only a quarter of the participating companies deemed that they had fully implemented all legal requirements. As a result, the competent data protection authorities were also rather cautious in their enforcement of violations and the associated possibility of imposing fines. To account for further developments in this domain, subsequent empirical studies will be necessary. In any event, the authors of this book should be congratulated for taking on this important work, which will hopefully inspire future research.

Munich, Germany   Michèle Finck
16 July 2019

Reference

Bitkom. (2018) *3 von 4 Unternehmen verfehlen die Frist der Datenschutz-Grundverordnung*, Pressemitteilung vom 17.05.2018, Bitkom e.V. Retrieved from https://www.bitkom.org/Presse/Presseinformation/3-von-4-Unternehmen-verfehlen-die-Frist-der-Datenschutz-Grundverordnung.html

Contents

About the Authors and the Project

Gregor Dorfleitner pursued graduate work in electrical engineering at the Baden-Wuerttemberg Cooperative State University Ravensburg and in mathematics and business administration at the University of Augsburg. He received his PhD in 1998 and subsequently completed his habilitation in the field of business administration in 2003 at the Faculty of Business and Economics of the same university. From 2004 until 2007, he was a full professor of finance at Vienna University of Economics and Business. Since 2007, he has held a chair in finance and has been the director of the Center of Finance at the University of Regensburg. Since 2010, he has been an associate researcher at the Centre for European Research in Microfinance (CERMi) in Belgium. He has published more than 60 articles in internationally renowned scientific journals. His research focuses on sustainable investments, microfinancing, and FinTech, among others. He has worked on numerous projects related to FinTechs, text analytics, and sustainable investments and has raised external funding for several scientific projects from the Deutsche Forschungsgemeinschaft, the Fritz Thyssen Stiftung, and the German Ministry of Finance. The WirtschaftsWoche ranked Gregor Dorfleitner in the category of lifetime achievement in the top 5% of researchers in business administration within the German-speaking area.

Lars Hornuf completed his PhD in economics at the Ludwig Maximilian University (LMU) of Munich in 2011 and subsequently received his habilitation in the field of business administration in 2019 at the University of Regensburg. Previously, he was a junior researcher at the Ifo Institute for Economic Research and a research associate at the Institute of International Law at LMU. He has been a visiting scholar at UC Berkeley, Stanford Law School, Duke University, Georgetown University, the CESifo, and the House of Finance at Goethe University Frankfurt. In 2014, he became an assistant professor of law and economics in the Department of Economics of Trier University. Since 2016, he has been an affiliated research fellow at the Max Planck Institute for Innovation and Competition. Recently, Lars Hornuf became a full professor of business administration specializing in the areas of financial services and financial technology at the University of Bremen and an affiliate member of the

CESifo Research Network. He has worked on numerous projects related to FinTechs and raised external funding from the Deutsche Forschungsgemeinschaft and the German Ministry of Finance, among others. His research interests include FinTech, law and finance, and behavioral science. Media including *The Economist* and *Foreign Policy* have reported on his research findings.

This book is mainly based on two studies (Dorfleitner and Hornuf, 2018a, 2018b). These studies are part of the ABIDA project and are supported with funds from the German Ministry of Education and Research (funding reference 0 1 I S 1 5 0 1 6 A–F). The content of the book solely reflects the opinions of the authors and does not necessarily reflect the views of the Ministry or those of the individual project partners. ABIDA explores social opportunities and risks of the generation, linking, and analysis of data and develops options for political action, research, and development.

References

Dorfleitner, G., & Hornuf, L. (2018a). Neue digitale Akteure und ihre Rolle in der Finanzwirtschaft: Eine Analyse des deutschen Marktes unter besonderer Berücksichtigung von Datenschutzaspekten. *ABIDA – Externe Gutachten.* Retrieved from https://epub.uni-regensburg.de/37203/1/Gutachten_ABIDA_Neue_Digitale_Akteure_Finanzwirtschaft.pdf
Dorfleitner, G., & Hornuf, L. (2018b). Analyse der Datenschutzerklärungen deutscher FinTech-Unternehmen nach Einführung der DSGVO. *ABIDA – Externe Gutachten.* Retrieved from http://www.abida.de/sites/default/files/ABIDA_Folgegutachten_Fintech_DSGVO.pdf

List of Figures

Chapter 1
Introduction

Abstract The chapter outlines the research questions and scope of the book. This book pursues three main objectives. First, we analyze the general perspectives of new digital players in the financial industry, the so-called FinTechs, in Germany. Second, we focus on the handling and use of user data by FinTechs. In this context, we analyze the privacy statements of 505 FinTechs active in Germany. Third, we examine additional questions related to the data processing of FinTechs, such as their business models, cooperation with banks, and regulatory issues. This chapter also provides a brief overview of the methods we apply throughout the book.

This book pursues three main objectives. First, we analyze the general perspectives of new digital players in the financial industry, the so-called FinTechs, in Germany. Second, we focus on FinTechs' handling and use of user data. In this context, we analyze the privacy statements of 505 FinTechs active in Germany. Third, we examine additional questions related to the data processing of FinTechs, including FinTech business models, the cooperation between FinTechs and banks, and regulatory issues.

To reach our three objectives, we proceed as follows. Chapter 2 provides an overview of the German FinTech market. We focus on the players that are active in Germany and their total market volumes. The analysis is based mainly on two of our recent publications about the German FinTech market (Dorfleitner et al. 2017, 2019). Chapter 3 constitutes the core of this book. We analyze how active FinTechs in Germany process user data. Moreover, we examine the following questions: How well do the FinTechs inform users of their services about the collection and use of personal data? What data do the FinTech companies operating in Germany process? With whom is the data shared? Chapter 4 examines the extent to which the processing of data changed after the implementation of the General Data Protection Regulation (GDPR). Chapter 5 focuses on four additional questions about FinTechs in Germany. Initially, we analyze and evaluate the forms of cooperation between banks and FinTechs. Moreover, we discuss the application and implementation of big data analytics in the FinTech market. We also examine whether the business models of FinTechs are sustainable and whether FinTechs can provide access to debt capital markets to companies, which have so far been denied such access, even

© Springer Nature Switzerland AG 2019

G. Dorfleitner, L. Hornuf, *FinTech and Data Privacy in Germany*,
https://doi.org/10.1007/978-3-030-31335-7_1

though they could have used the additional debt to invest in profitable projects. Finally, Chap. 6 discusses the regulation of the German FinTech market.

Methodologically, this book uses different data sources. In addition to the investigation of scientific publications, we conducted 36 interviews with relevant experts of different stakeholder groups. These experts include executives of several FinTechs, traditional financial institutions, leading consultancies and law firms, various research institutes, regulatory authorities, and associations. Appendix A.1 provides an overview of the interviewees. We assured all respondents that the interviews would be evaluated and presented anonymously. For this reason, most of the answers represent the opinion of the interviewee and not the opinion of the institution for which the experts work. Answers should be interpreted accordingly. Furthermore, the accuracy of the statements cannot be verified for all experts, and therefore the answers represent the assessments and opinions of the respondents only. Nevertheless, the expert interviews allow deep insights into a range of topics and FinTech segments. We thank all the respondents for their time and valuable conversations. The interviews used a structured questionnaire, which is presented in Appendix A.2. The mean interview duration was more than 1 h, with the majority of interviews carried out by telephone; three interviews were held personally. Two experts completed the questionnaire autonomously and sent the results by e-mail. The findings of the interviews are incorporated in the text in the appropriate passages.

The chapters and subchapters in this book mostly follow a uniform structure. We begin with an overview of the applicable literature. Given the variety of topics and FinTech segments, we do not claim comprehensiveness. Instead, we present the most recent and relevant arguments and results. Subsequently, we provide an analysis of the processed data in the form of expert interviews or an investigation of the privacy statements. Each chapter ends with a short summary and conclusion.

References

Dorfleitner, G., Hornuf, L., Schmitt, M., & Weber, M. (2017). *FinTech in Germany*. Cham: Springer International.

Dorfleitner, G., Hornuf, L., Schmitt, M., & Weber, M. (2019). Marktüberblick. In F. Möslein & S. Omlor (Eds.), *FinTech-Handbuch. Digitalisierung, Recht, Finanzen* (pp. 21–38). Munich: C.H.Beck.

Chapter 2
Players in the German FinTech Industry

Abstract This chapter analyzes the development and current status of the German FinTech market. In particular, it outlines the different segments and subsegments of the FinTech industry. It further provides descriptive statistics on market volume for each segment, discusses general trends, and analyzes current market developments.

This chapter presents the development and current status of the German FinTech market. The insights are based mainly on two publications, namely Dorfleitner et al. (2017, 2019).

Apart from online banking, which has existed in Germany since the 1980s, the German financial sector has long resisted digitalization. Only in the past few years have new digital financial services such as crowdfunding arisen. These financial services are frequently provided by independent companies that are mostly in their start-up phase or those that have passed their start-up phase only recently. These firms are also called FinTech companies or FinTechs for short. FinTechs provide a wide range of financial services (see Fig. 2.1).

In the remainder of this chapter, we describe the FinTech segments and subsegments, after which we report on the exact number of FinTechs and volume in the particular subsegments. Subsequently, we discuss several general developments and trends in the FinTech sector.

2.1 Segments of the FinTech Industry

The first segment, finance, includes the large subsegment crowdfunding. In general, crowdfunding describes a form of financing a project or a business in which several contributors each provide only a part of the funding amount (Klöhn and Hornuf 2012). Usually, FinTechs in this segment operate platforms to bring together the projects and the contributors (i.e., *the crowd*). There are four different forms of crowdfunding. While investors in donation-based crowdfunding do not receive any material benefits, in rewards-based crowdfunding they receive nonmonetary material compensation or pre-purchase a product or service. In crowdlending, a loan

© Springer Nature Switzerland AG 2019

G. Dorfleitner, L. Hornuf, *FinTech and Data Privacy in Germany*,

https://doi.org/10.1007/978-3-030-31335-7_2

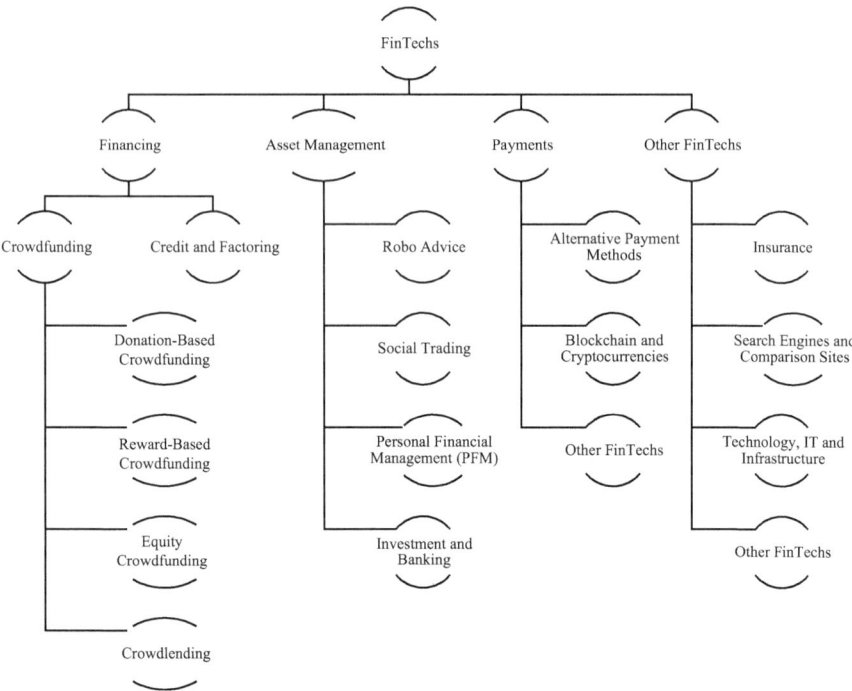

Fig. 2.1 FinTech segments. Source: Dorfleitner et al. (2017)

is funded by the crowd. After the funding, the loan is paid back with predefined interest payments and a predefined duration (Dorfleitner et al. 2017). De facto, crowdlending platforms create marketplaces for loans, which are sometimes funded by only a few and partly professional investors. For this reason, the term *marketplace lending* to describe this form of financing is common as well. The fourth crowdfunding form, equity crowdfunding, is most similar to equity capital financing (Klöhn and Hornuf 2012). However, equity crowdfunding in Germany mostly constitutes mezzanine or debt financing, in which investors participate in the success of the project or business. Seldom do investors receive control rights comparable to those of real equity investments (Hornuf et al. 2018).

Other FinTechs in the finance segment provide several forms of loans and loan substitutes, which are usually not refinanced by a crowd of investors but by a bank. This subsegment includes, among others, platforms that arrange loans or factoring services (Dorfleitner and Rad 2017). Some FinTechs in this subsegment focus explicitly on small and medium-sized enterprises because, for these companies, forms of alternative finance are particularly important (Gomber et al. 2017).

Second, FinTechs in the segment of asset management offer investment advice, wealth management, and active asset management. The subsegment of social trading comprises FinTechs that create transparent marketplaces on which investors can observe the portfolio strategies of a large number of other investors (i.e., *the signal providers*). The FinTechs also provide the possibility to conveniently follow these signal providers, and automatically copy the transactions and portfolio decisions for the investor, if desired (Dorfleitner et al. 2017). While investment strategies are made by humans in social trading, they are automated by FinTechs in the robo advice subsegment. Transactions are initiated by algorithms. In general, one can distinguish between a one-time automated investment advice and a continuous portfolio management through algorithms (Dorfleitner et al. 2017). However, the borders between these two alternatives blur in reality. FinTechs in the subsegment of personal financial management offer app-based or software-based solutions to facilitate private financial planning, particularly the presentation and administration of financial assets and finance flows (Dorfleitner et al. 2017). Thus, FinTechs in this subsegment provide a user-friendly presentation of financial assets and sometimes also advisory functions; however, in contrast with other subsegments in the asset management segment, they do not offer automated portfolio management. Many FinTechs in the personal financial management subsegment use application programming interfaces (APIs) to access banking data with the consent of the customer of the personal financial management services (Dorfleitner et al. 2017). FinTechs that support asset management and that are not part of the three previously described subsegments are included in the investment and banking subsegment. This subsegment comprises, for example, deposit brokers, which arrange daily or fixed-term deposits in foreign countries and offer the opening and management on a German website. Furthermore, FinTechs that offer asset management and incorporate both automated processes and human interaction belong to this subsegment. Finally, the investment and banking subsegment describes FinTechs that offer traditional banking products, such as a checking account, with certain user-friendly functionalities. FinTechs in the asset management sector frequently possess adequate licenses (e.g., an asset management license, a banking license) in case the business requires such an authorization.

The third segment, payment, includes FinTechs that offer alternative payment methods such as mobile payments, peer-to-peer payments, instant payments, and e-wallets (Dorfleitner et al. 2017). Another subsegment of payments comprises providers of cryptocurrencies, services associated with cryptocurrencies, and blockchain applications connected with finance. FinTechs in the payment segment, such as apps to split a restaurant bill among friends, rarely belong to either the first or the second subsegment. These FinTechs are thus classified in the subsegment of other payment FinTechs. All remaining FinTechs that are not included in one of these three described segments are classified as other FinTechs. The subsegment insurance includes FinTechs that offer diverse insurance services. Another subsegment includes FinTechs that focus on search engines and the comparison of financial products. Finally, FinTechs that provide solutions for technical, IT, and infrastructure issues for financial service providers are classified in their own subsegment. This last subsegment includes all remaining FinTechs that cannot be included in any other segment or subsegment. As previously mentioned, this systematization follows the approach of Dorfleitner et al. (2017).

The list of German FinTechs used by Dorfleitner et al. (2019) is also used in this book. A closer analysis of the sample of the 505 FinTechs indicates that most can be clearly classified into the previously described subsegments. However, several FinTechs offer various services and thus can be included in several subsegments. In the context of this book, we classify these FinTechs into subsegments according to their primary or historically established services. Moreover, several FinTechs own a banking license and thus can be regarded as banks, even though they are still in their start-up phase with respect to their founding date. In addition, several traditional financial institutions offer FinTech services. These are included in the classification as long as their services are offered by the subsidiary. If the FinTech application is incorporated in the bank or the mobile or online presence of the bank, the FinTech service can still be classified into subsegments, but it is not possible to identify a corresponding FinTech company.

2.2 The German Market

According to the classification described in Sect. 2.1, we divide the underlying sample of 505 FinTechs into segments and subsegments. Figure 2.2 presents the corresponding allocation.

As the figure shows, payment is the largest subsegment, with 104 FinTechs, while only 15 FinTechs fall in the crowdlending subsegment. However, these numbers provide only minimal evidence on the importance of the segments. In particular, the payment segment contains many FinTechs that offer diverse mobile and instant payment technologies. The respective FinTechs only account for small market shares, and many are not likely to establish themselves in the market. By contrast,

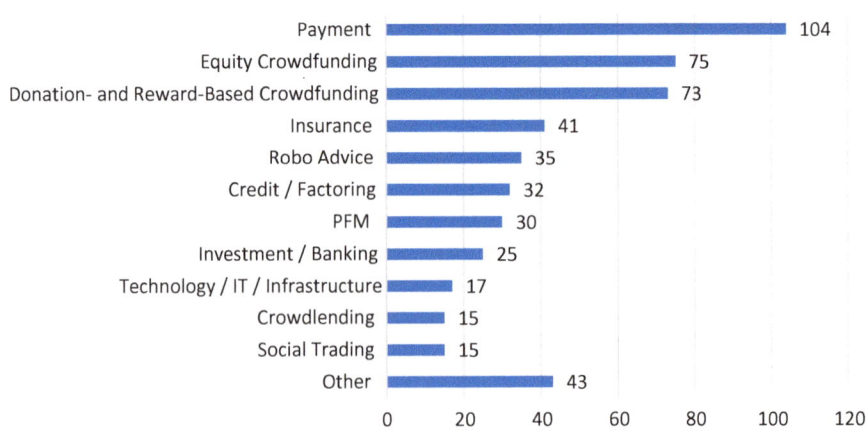

Fig. 2.2 FinTechs in Germany by segments. Source: Dorfleitner et al. (2019)

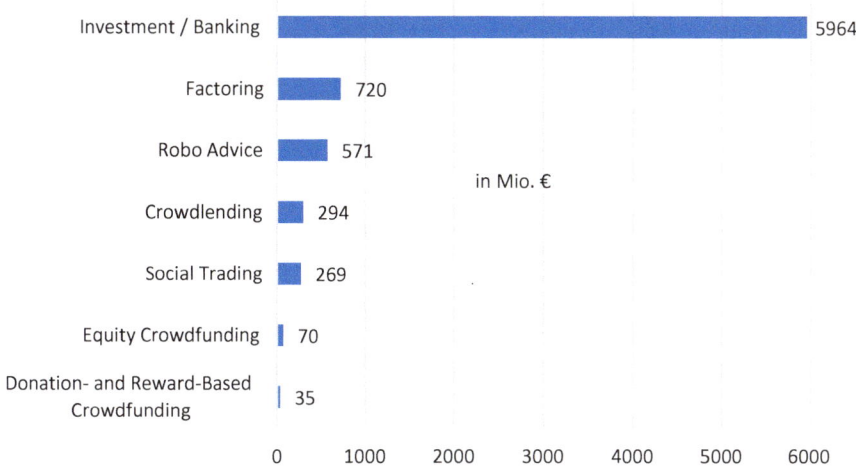

Fig. 2.3 Volume of selected FinTech segments in 2016. Source: Dorfleitner et al. (2019)

the crowdlending segment is one of the most mature FinTech segments in Germany,[1] and the market has already concentrated accordingly.

Therefore, the volume of mediated financial services is more meaningful to assess the importance of the segments. Relevant volume is estimated by Dorfleitner et al. (2019). Figure 2.3 shows the market volumes in 2016, at least for selected sub-segments. Note that assets under management represent the market volume in asset management, while market volumes are measured by the financing volume in the finance segment. The market volume grew from 2015 to 2016, with the highest growth rate being recorded in the segment of asset management. The growth is likely attributable to the lasting zero interest rate environment in Germany, which encourages investors to invest their money in daily fixed-term deposits in foreign countries via respective platforms. In this way, investments yield at least a small one-digit interest rate. Compared with 2015, many investors decided in favor of these investments in 2016, which resulted in a growth rate of around 500% over 2015 (Dorfleitner et al. 2019).

Although the FinTech segments continue to grow, it is important to note that the respective volume only represents a small fraction of the respective total markets (Dorfleitner et al. 2017). The importance of FinTechs is thus justified not by their recent market shares but by their future potential.

Dorfleitner et al. (2017) project the future development in the subsegments until 2035 by deriving three different scenarios: an optimistic, a real case, and a pessimistic scenario. The scenarios are based on several assumptions about future conditions, such as regulation. The analysis of the real-case scenario suggests that many segments are likely to grow substantially. Dorfleitner et al. (2017) estimate that the

---

[1]The current market leader auxmoney entered the market in 2008.

total volume of the finance and asset management segments will grow to 148 billion euros in 2035 in the real-case scenario. The optimistic scenario projects the total market volume of the two segments to amount to 847 billion euros in 2035. The asset management sector accounts for 105 billion euros in the real-case scenario and 600 billion euros in the optimistic scenario for the majority of the projected volume. In the finance sector, particularly the volumes of FinTechs active in factoring, loan brokering, or crowdlending are expected to grow, while the other forms of crowdfunding are projected to remain below a financing volume of 1 billion euros in the real-case scenario. Dorfleitner et al. (2019) do not estimate the market volume of FinTechs in the payment sector; however, Dorfleitner et al. (2017) estimated this volume to amount to around 17 billion euros in 2015. The majority of the payment services offered by FinTechs are applicable in online shopping,[2] and the market for online shopping grew with a rate of 10.8% in 2015 (Handelsverband Deutschland 2017). Thus, we estimate that the volume of alternative payment methods in Germany amounted to 18.8 billion euros in 2016.

2.3   General Market Trends

In general, the literature on the German FinTech market agrees that all FinTech segments are growing and are likely to grow even more in the future. Dorfleitner et al. (2017) highlight the importance of regulatory circumstances and the implementation of Brexit for future development. Both topics appear undisputable, and we discuss regulatory issues in more detail later in this book.

On January 13, 2018, the revised Payment Services Supervision Act (*Zahlungsdiensteaufsichtsgesetz*) became binding in Germany, with the purpose of turning the regulations of the Second Payment Services Directive (RL (EU) 2015/2366) of January 2016 into national law. The Second Payment Services Directive provides regulations on the extent to which bank data must be made available to account information service providers and payment initiation service providers in case the customer (i.e., the holder of the respective bank account) agrees to the passing of data. As a result, banks lose a crucial advantage over FinTechs because now they can no longer solely control the bank data of their clients. The Directive is also important for FinTechs because they now have the opportunity to develop new services based on the available customer data. Overall, the Second Payment Services Directive not only is a regulatory measure but also is of importance in the context of data issues and for business models of some FinTechs.

In analyzing the 38 expert interviews regarding FinTechs in Germany that we conducted in the scope of this book, we can derive further general market trends.

---

[2]We only consider alternative payments here. According to Thiele and Diehl (2017) cryptocurrencies are not often used for the payment of goods or services.

These trends include both opportunities and threats and are shortly described in what follows.

At present, established financial institutions are often perceived as innovation averse. In this context, FinTechs appear to be the opponents of traditional banks; however, cooperation between these two players already exists. In a few years, some FinTechs might gain relevant market shares and become banks themselves by obtaining a banking license. Many FinTech functionalities could be integrated into the business model of established banks either through the reproduction of the respective solution by the bank or through acquisitions or close cooperation with the FinTechs. In the long run, integration of the seemingly opponent systems appears probable.

Many FinTechs active on today's market do not have enough unique selling points and cannot create sufficient customer value to survive in the long run. Moreover, some areas, such as in mobile payment, have several technical solutions. However, in the end only one or a few solutions are likely to prevail. This implies a further consolidation of the market.

In any case, digital financial services will play an increasingly important role in the future and will heavily shape the financial sector, regardless of the number of FinTechs in the future. Without doubt, FinTechs, traditional banks, and big-tech companies will offer many digital financial services. There are already many indications that established digital companies such as Alibaba, Amazon.com, Apple, Facebook, Google, and Tencent are extending their services in the finance sector (Dapp 2015). In this context, Zetzsche et al. (2018) call these companies TechFins, as they mainly focus on data collection and technology. Financial services are added as another offer to existing users. Traditional comparison sites such as Check24 and Verivox are also implementing FinTech applications, such as deposit brokering, insurance services, or personal financial management tools (Dohms 2017). Verivox has recently taken over the insolvent FinTech Outbank and now plans to screen checking accounts for overcharged contracts. In this way, Verivox wants to become a digital financial assistant. As these players already have large numbers of customers who trust the respective company and owing to network externalities, it is possible that these companies and the traditional financial institutions and FinTechs can ultimately share the market for digital financial services.

The extent to which FinTechs have shaped and are still shaping the digitalization of financial services through technical innovations remains questionable in terms of scale. In the expert interviews, we raised the question: "Which general technological innovations (not business model innovations) have FinTechs developed" (question 4 in Appendix A.2). Figure 2.4 presents the results of the expert interviews. While every fifth expert indicated that FinTechs essentially do not account for any innovation, the other experts named the following innovations attributable to FinTechs:

- Online and app-based payment services in online shopping allow instant activation of a money transfer and also instantly notify the merchant accordingly. This procedure speeds up the online shopping process. In Fig. 2.4, these payment services are represented in the category *instant payments*.

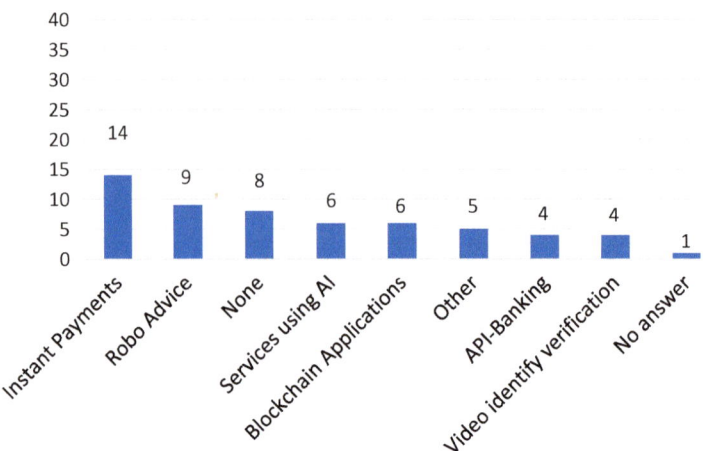

Fig. 2.4 Answers to the question of technical innovations by FinTechs (Multiple choices possible)

- *Robo advice* facilitates a new kind of asset management. The use of algorithms in portfolio management allows easier investment decisions usually using exchange-traded funds. The FinTechs Ginmon, Scalable Capital, and Vaamo are the pioneers in this area.
- *Video identity verification* allows customers to complete all financial services online without having to go to a branch for legitimization. The FinTechs IDnow and WebID are regarded as the pioneers in this area. IDnow even patented the video identity verification process in 2016 under the patent EP 2948891 B1.
- Six experts mentioned *blockchain applications* and services using artificial intelligence (AI). An example of the latter is automated credit risk models.
- *Other innovations* include the home banking computer interface standard and the screening of bills.

Some experts stressed that FinTechs often alter financial services by digitizing existing financial services and designing them in more user-friendly ways. FinTechs also offer increasingly more back-office applications for the business-to-business (B2B) sector.

According to an expert, an advantage of FinTechs is that they use customer data more completely and more comprehensively. Client advisers in traditional banks often use customer data only erratically and incompletely. Thus, a more comprehensive use of data by FinTechs means better service for customers. Moreover, a more complete use of data leads to increased efficiency and greater customer proximity. Some experts, however, emphasized that FinTech services are often a combination of existing services and methods and do not constitute genuine development.

Many experts also noted that FinTechs use, adapt, and develop other technologies such as big data applications, AI, open API, or distributed ledgers (six mentions).

However, these technologies have not been invented by FinTechs and are also used in other contexts.

To sum up the topic of technical innovations, FinTechs most often act evolutionary instead of revolutionary and adopt many innovations they did not originally invent themselves, such as the blockchain technology. However, these innovations are perceived to be attributed to FinTechs.

While we extensively explore opportunities of and threats to FinTechs regarding the topics of data protection, cooperation with banks, business models, and impact on the real economy later in this book, this chapter concludes with a general discussion on the opportunities for and threats to FinTechs.

An advantage of the mostly innovative FinTechs is that they provide easily usable, completely digital solutions with a stronger focus on the needs of customers of financial services. Moreover, in cases in which the new solutions replace already-existing services, complete digitalization creates a more cost-efficient offer. After all, as mentioned, many FinTechs offer solutions that already exist, but they require less minimum volume. For example, FinTechs in the factoring subsegment also offer factoring of particular invoices to small enterprises, which do not have a large annual turnover. The latter property is also called *scaling down*.

The risks customers of FinTechs are facing are obvious as well. As FinTechs are usually in their start-up phase, many potential users do not know whether the respective company will still exist in a few years, whether the FinTech has enough resources for data security and data protection, and whether the solutions indeed work in the way the FinTechs are promising. Furthermore, systematic risks may arise, such as when a robo advice FinTech invests the money of many customers completely in the same way. In this case, the decision to sell a particular security for all customers may result in a price drop of the respective security. So far, this risk is purely theoretical, as is the threat of a new financial crisis from the securitization of loans of debtors with poor creditworthiness, which are mediated by FinTechs.

From a bank's perspective, a potential risk in this context is that FinTechs will significantly cannibalize business or at least cause a reduction of the feasible margins in the market. As a consequence, previous revenue models may not work any longer. However, this represents an opportunity for users of financial services.

References

Dapp, T.-F. (2015). *Fintech reloaded—Traditional banks as digital ecosystems: With proven walled garden strategies into the future*. Frankfurt am Main: Deutsche Bank Research.

Dohms, H.-R. (2017). *Exklusiv: Verivox schluckt Outbank—und will jetzt Fintechs und Banken attackieren*. Retrieved from Finanz-Szene.de: http://finanz-szene.de/exklusiv-verivox-schluckt-outbank-und-will-jetzt-fintechs-und-banken-attackieren/

Dorfleitner, G., & Rad, J. (2017). Wie FinTechs den Factoring-Markt neu gestalten. *Corporate Finance, 2017*, 358–363.

Dorfleitner, G., Hornuf, L., Schmitt, M., & Weber, M. (2017). *FinTech in Germany*. Cham: Springer International.

Dorfleitner, G., Hornuf, L., Schmitt, M., & Weber, M. (2019). Marktüberblick. In F. Möslein & S. Omlor (Eds.), *FinTech-Handbuch. Digitalisierung, Recht, Finanzen* (pp. 21–38). Munich: C.H.Beck.

Gomber, P., Koch, J.-A., & Siering, M. (2017). Mittelstandsfinanzierung im Kontext von FinTech und Digital Finance. *Corporate Finance, 2017,* 327–332.

Handelsverband Deutschland (2017). *Handel digital: Online-monitor 2017.* Berlin: HDE.

Hornuf, L., Klöhn, L., & Schilling, T. (2018). Financial contracting in crowdinvesting: Lessons from the German market. *German Law Journal, 19*(3), 509–578.

Klöhn, L., & Hornuf, L. (2012). Crowdinvesting in Deutschland: Markt, Rechtslage und Regulierungsperspektiven. *Zeitschrift für Bankenrecht und Bankwirtschaft, 24,* 237–266.

Thiele, C.-L., & Diehl, M. (2017). Kryptowährung Bitcoin: Währungswettbewerb oder Spekulationsobjekt: Welche Konsequenzen sind für das aktuelle Geldsystem zu erwarten? *ifo Schnelldienst, 70*(22), 3–6.

Zetzsche, D. A., Buckley, R., Arner, D., & Barberis, J. N. (2018). From FinTech to TechFin: The regulatory challenges of data-driven finance. *NYU Journal of Law and Business, 14*(2), 393–446.

Chapter 3
FinTechs and Data Protection

Abstract This chapter deals with data protection regarding FinTech services and how FinTechs dealt with it before the implementation of the GDPR in May 2018. The primary source of information on how FinTechs handled data protection is the privacy statements of the respective companies. We analyze these privacy statements with regard to three questions: What user data were processed? To whom were these data forwarded? And, if applicable, which third parties provided further information? In a second step, we conducted 36 expert interviews regarding the implementation of data protection and raised the question whether banks take a leap of faith with respect to data protection compared with FinTechs.

This chapter deals with the data protection regarding FinTech services before the implementation of the GDPR in May 2018. The primary source of information regarding the handling of data protection of FinTechs is the privacy statements of the respective companies. In a first step, we analyze these privacy statements in terms of three questions: What user data were processed? To whom were these data forwarded? And, if applicable, which third parties provided further information? In a second step, we asked the experts about specific data protection risks of FinTechs. In particular, we raised questions about the implementation of data protection in the scope of FinTechs and whether banks take a leap of faith with respect to data protection compared with FinTechs.

The Federal Data Protection Act (BDSG), which regulates the handling of personal data, and the Telemedia Act, which stipulates crucial regulations for Internet rights, form the legal framework for the processing of data in Germany. The BDSG enacted the European Data Protection Directive (RL 95/46/EG) into national law. Since May 25, 2018, the GDPR has been directly applicable in all EU member countries. In the following analysis, we refer to both the BDSG and the GDPR, as the underlying data in this chapter were collected before the GDPR became binding. The analysis in Chap. 4 focuses exclusively on the GDPR.

According to § 34 "Right of access by the data subject" of the BSDG, users of FinTech services have the right to information about the personal data processed by the FinTech. In this context, "data subjects" are natural persons whose personal data are processed according to the BDSG. FinTechs in general comply with this

G. Dorfleitner, L. Hornuf, *FinTech and Data Privacy in Germany*,
https://doi.org/10.1007/978-3-030-31335-7_3

regulation by publishing a privacy statement. To gain further information on what user data were processed, to whom these data were forwarded, and which third parties were asked for additional information about the data subject, we systematically collected and analyzed the privacy statements of FinTechs between October 15, 2017, and December 20, 2017. Therefore, we use the same sample of FinTechs Dorfleitner et al. (2019) examine.

Sixty-five of the 505 FinTechs analyzed by Dorfleitner et al. (2019) had no website and, thus, no privacy statement available. Another 65 FinTechs had a website; however, despite extensive research on the website, we could not find any privacy statement online. To ensure that the missing websites and privacy statements were not just a temporary issue of the FinTechs, we repeated the online search 3 weeks later. We found that 50 FinTechs did not present the privacy statement as a separate document but incorporated it on the imprint page ($N = 18$), in the disclaimer ($N = 3$), in the legal section ($N = 19$), as an index ($N = 6$), or in the terms of use ($N = 4$). Overall, we found a separate or integrated privacy statement on the websites of 375 FinTechs. Analysis of the particular FinTech segments as shown in Fig. 3.1 indicates that FinTechs in the subsegments credit and factoring (91%, $N = 29$) most often provided a privacy statement. By contrast, privacy statements were least common in personal financial management (63%, $N = 19$), donation- and reward-based crowdfunding (66%, $N = 48$), and social trading (67%, $N = 10$).

On average, the privacy statements were five A4 pages long (min.: <1 page; max.: 37 pages) and contained 1840 words (min.: 20 words; max.: 14,672 words). Assuming a reading speed of 250 words per minute as used by McDonald and Cranor (2009), the time to read an average privacy statement was slightly more than 7 min. However, i t takes users almost an hour to read the longest privacy statement. In this book, we did not analyze the readability of the privacy statements; however, the statements varied greatly in terms of this topic as well. While some privacy statements extensively used passive constructions and very long sentences, other FinTechs made a great effort to write them as easily understandable as possible.[1]

In total, 16 FinTechs explicitly stated that the processing of personal data is based on a different legislation than the German law. As Fig. 3.2 shows, the English, the Swiss, and the Luxembourg law were especially popular. The majority of companies that did not refer to foreign law often referenced German law.[2] Regarding the processing of personal data, several FinTech companies also referred to codes of conduct, which several industries such as the German insurance sector have enacted.

---

[1]For example, the privacy statement of OptioPay states (originally in German, translation by the authors): "We have tried to formulate the privacy statement as understandable, transparent, and easy as possible. Persons without legal and technical knowledge should be able to understand the content without problems. Should you have, against expectations, any problems understanding the privacy statement, feel free to contact us via support@optiopay.com."

[2]For example, the privacy statement of Founderio states (originally in German, translation by the authors): "Founderio is subject to the Federal Data Protection Act (BDSG), the Telemedia Act (TMG), and the General Data Protection Regulation (EU)."

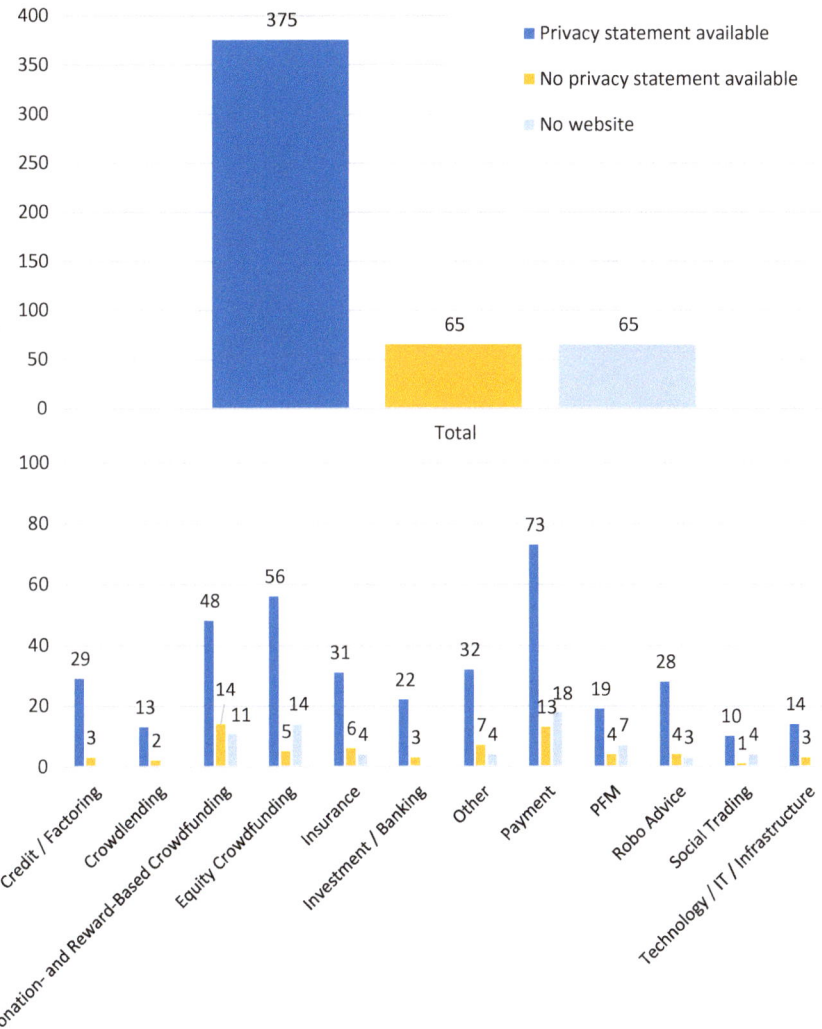

Fig. 3.1 Frequency of using a privacy statement. Distinction according to FinTech segment, $N = 505$

The great majority of the FinTech companies (94%, $N = 352$) stated that they process personal data. None of the FinTechs explicitly mentioned not processing personal data, and 6% ($N = 23$) did not specify in the privacy statement what type of data they process. Fairly often, further information about the type of processed data was missing in the privacy statements, especially in the segments credit and factoring (10%, $N = 3$), social trading (10%, $N = 1$), and donation- and reward-based crowdfunding (8%, $N = 4$). Figure 3.3 shows the respective allocation.

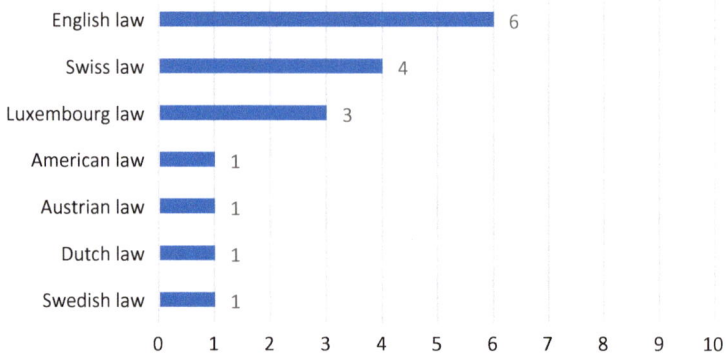

Fig. 3.2 Law applicable to data processing if a foreign law was explicitly mentioned. Number of evaluated privacy statements $N = 375$

Moreover, analysis of the privacy statements reveals that the majority of FinTechs that provide a privacy statement did not exhaustively list the types of personal data that were processed. By contrast, 56% ($N = 209$) of the privacy statements used examples and phrases such as "for example," "possibly," and "among others." As Fig. 3.4 shows, 38% ($N = 23$) of the FinTechs provided a conclusive list of the processed data. However, 6% ($N = 23$) of the privacy statements did not include any information on what personal data are processed. Often, FinTechs in the segments crowdlending (69%, $N = 9$) and insurance (48%, $N = 15$) provided a complete list of the processed personal data. Almost half the FinTechs in the payment sector provided an incomplete list of what personal data are processed by the company.

After analyzing whether FinTechs specifically listed the types of personal data they process, we examine in a second step why 209 privacy statements did not include a conclusive list. Figure 3.5 shows that the majority of these FinTechs only used examples of personal data they process (57%, $N = 120$). Another 22% ($N = 47$) referred to a legal definition,[3] explaining what personal data are, and the remaining 20% ($N = 42$) only stated that these types of data are processed by the FinTech. Mentioning examples was particularly popular in the subsegment investment and banking. Privacy statements of FinTechs in the subsegments robo advice and credit and factoring often included a legal definition. FinTechs in the subsegments social trading, credit and factoring, and donation- and reward-based crowdfunding most often noted in their privacy statement only that they process personal data.

As of September 2009, the BDSG defined in § 3 "Further definitions" personal data as *"any information concerning the personal or material circumstances of an*

---

[3]For example, the privacy statement of the FinTech Zinsbaustein uses the following legal definition (originally in German, translation by the authors): "Subject to data protection is personal data. According to § 3 Sec. 1 BDSG, personal data refer to any information about the personal or material circumstances of an identified or identifiable natural person. This includes information such as the name, the address, the e-mail address or phone number, and, where appropriate, usage data."

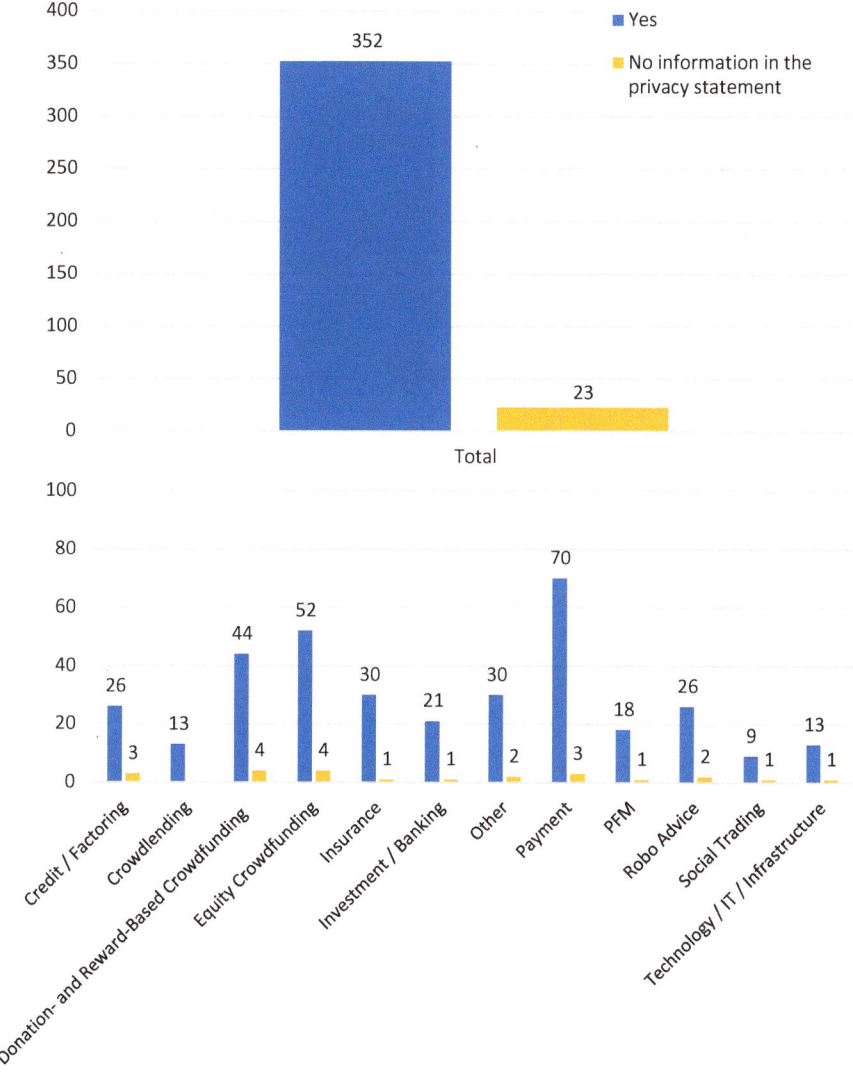

Fig. 3.3 Frequency of privacy statements noting that personal or personally identifiable information is being processed. Distinction according to FinTech segment $N = 375$

identified or identifiable natural person ('data subject')" (translation by the authors). Particular pieces of information such as name, phone number, credit, or personnel number are usually clearly associated with a particular person and therefore constitute personal data. Processed data are also related to persons if the reference to a particular person can be made indirectly. For example, if there is only one single-family house on a street, the address already constitutes personal data.

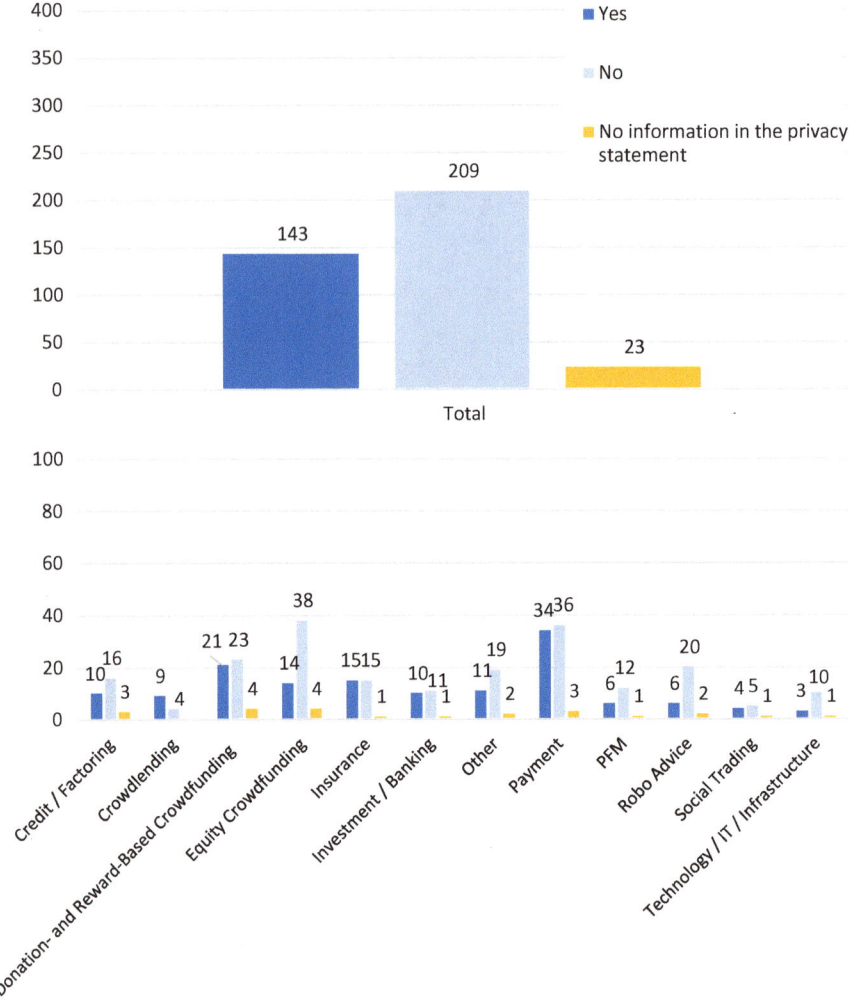

Fig 3.4 Frequency of privacy statements that note what personal data are processed. Distinction according to FinTech segment $N = 375$

In Article 4 "Definitions," the GDPR does not distinguish between personal and material circumstances; however, the definition of personal data is similar to the legal definition of the BDSG. The GDPR defines personal data as "*any information relating to an identified or identifiable natural person ('data subject'); an identifiable natural person is one who can be identified, directly or indirectly, in particular by reference to an identifier such as a name, an identification number, location data, an online identifier or to one or more factors specific to the physical, physiological, genetic, mental, economic, cultural or social identity of that natural person.*" While an identified person refers to specific information about a particular known person,

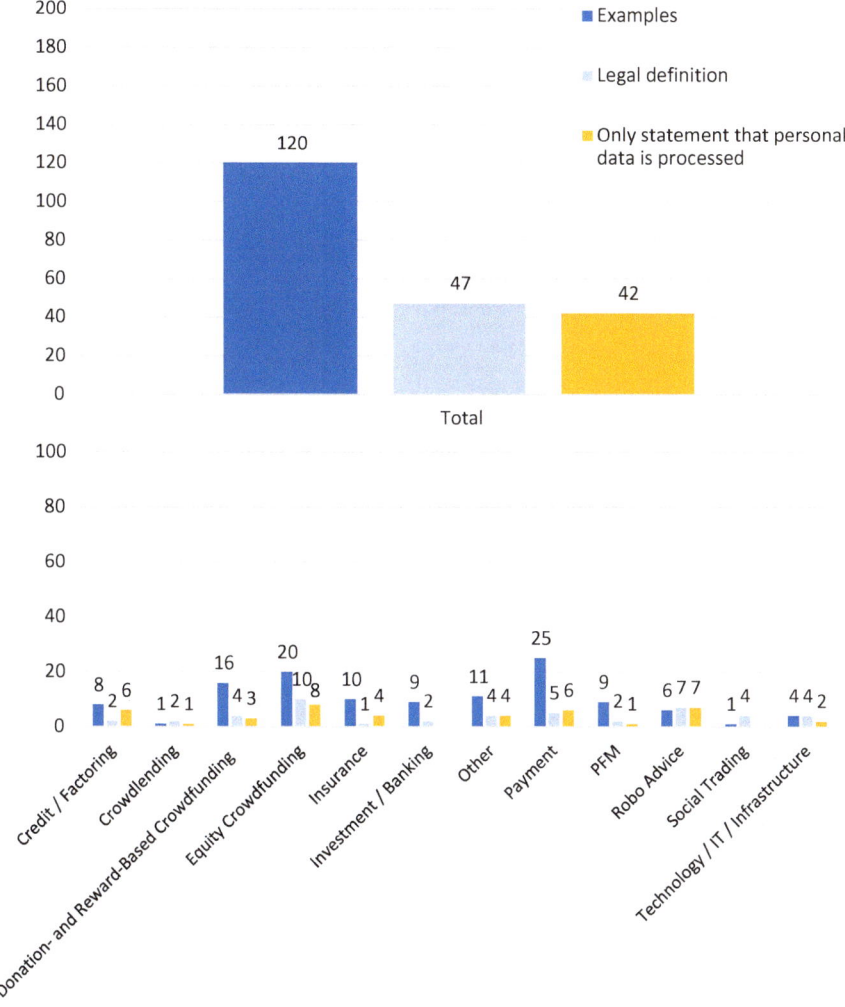

Fig. 3.5 Reasons that personal data were not listed exhaustively. Distinction according to FinTech segment, $N = 209$

an identifiable person refers to information that could identify a person indirectly. For example, according to Article 4 GDPR, the location data, an online identifier, or one or more factors specific to the physical, physiological, genetic, mental, economic, cultural, or social identity could help identify a person indirectly.

In the following analysis, we examine the privacy statements regarding the specifically listed types of data the FinTechs processed according to their privacy statements. We find that most privacy statements listed data such as the name (64%, $N = 241$), the e-mail address (59%, $N = 222$), the address (55%, $N = 205$), and the phone number (33%, $N = 122$) as data the FinTech processed. This is followed by

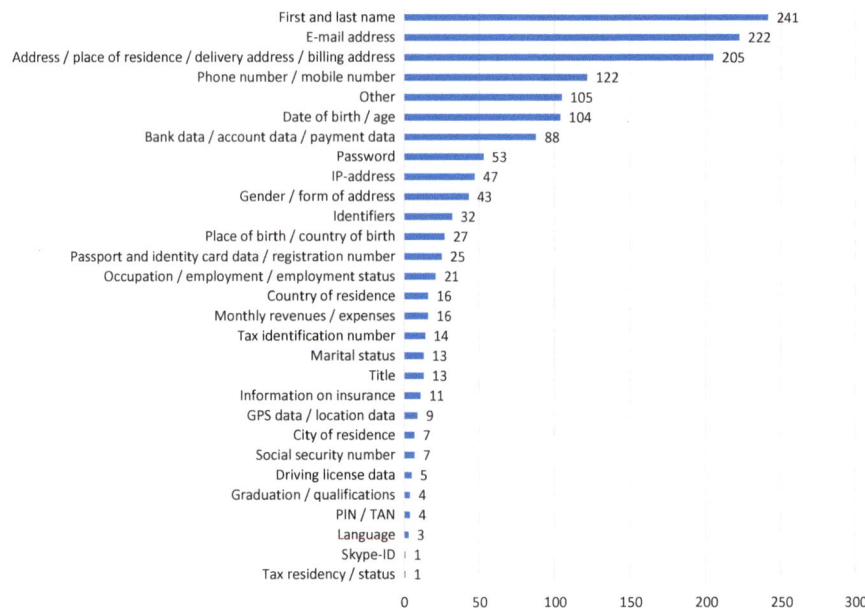

Fig. 3.6 Types of personal data processed according to the privacy statement. Number of evaluated privacy statements $N = 375$

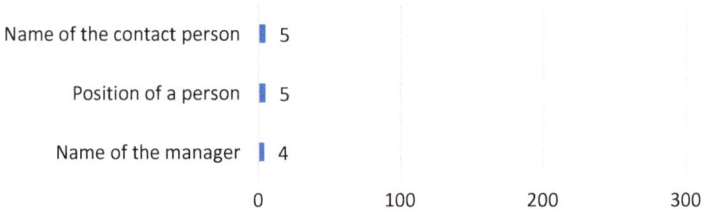

Fig. 3.7 Types of personal data collected in a company context that are processed according to the privacy statement. Number of evaluated privacy statements $N = 375$

the category other information (28%, $N = 105$), the age (28%, $N = 104$), account and payment data (23%, $N = 88$), password (14%, $N = 53$), and IP address (13%, $N = 47$). Figure 3.6 shows the allocation of data categories for the entire German FinTech market. At least 25 FinTechs stated that they process ID card or passport data as well as the respective registration numbers, 21 mentioned the processing of information about the occupational situation, and nine stated that they process GPS and location data.

Furthermore, Fig. 3.7 shows that personal data were processed in a company context. In particular, the privacy statements explicitly mentioned processing data regarding the positions of people in a company, the name of a contact person, and the name of the manager. However, in general, this category was quite rare, and

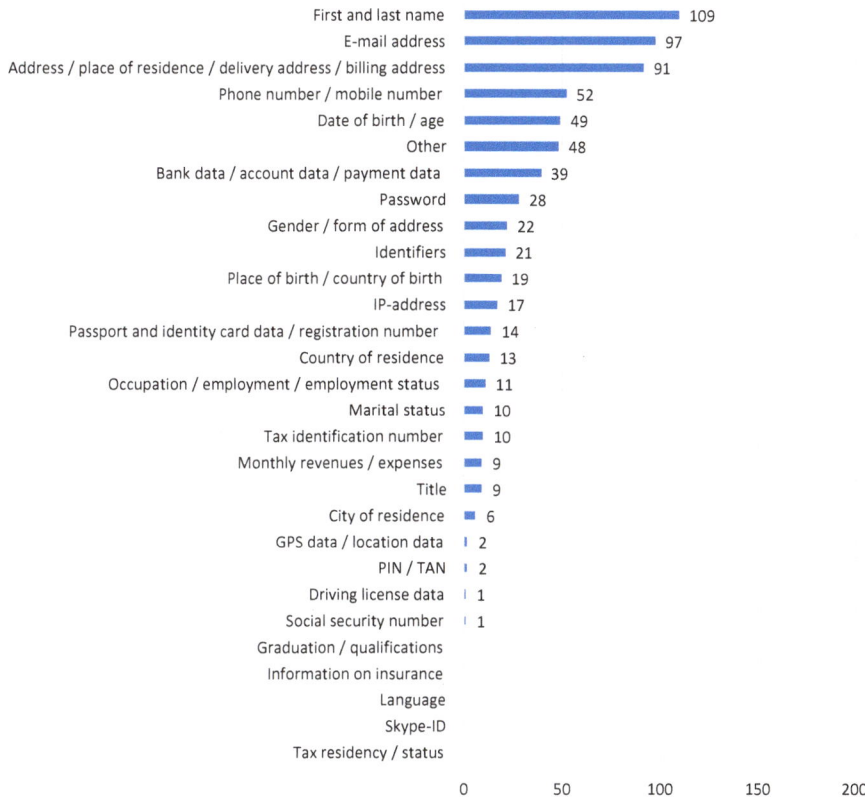

Fig. 3.8 Types of personal data processed according to the privacy statement in the financing segment. Number of evaluated privacy statements $N = 220$

therefore, in the following, we do not break down the numbers for the particular FinTech segments.

The specifically listed personal data differ among the FinTech segments. For a more detailed analysis, in Figs. 3.8, 3.9, 3.10, 3.11, and 3.12, we sum up the subsegments to the segments listed in Fig. 2.1: *payment*, *financing* (investment and banking, donation- and reward-based crowdfunding, equity crowdfunding, crowdlending, and credit and factoring), *asset management* (personal financial management, robo advice, and social trading), *insurance* (insurance), and *other FinTechs* (technology, IT and Infrastructure, and other FinTechs). In the figures, the *x*-axis is scaled down to the population of FinTechs in the respective segment. In all but one segment, the name remained the most common type of data processed. Only in the segment other FinTechs was the e-mail address more popular than the name. The e-mail address was the second most common data type in all other segments except asset management. In the segment asset management, the address was more often processed than the e-mail address.

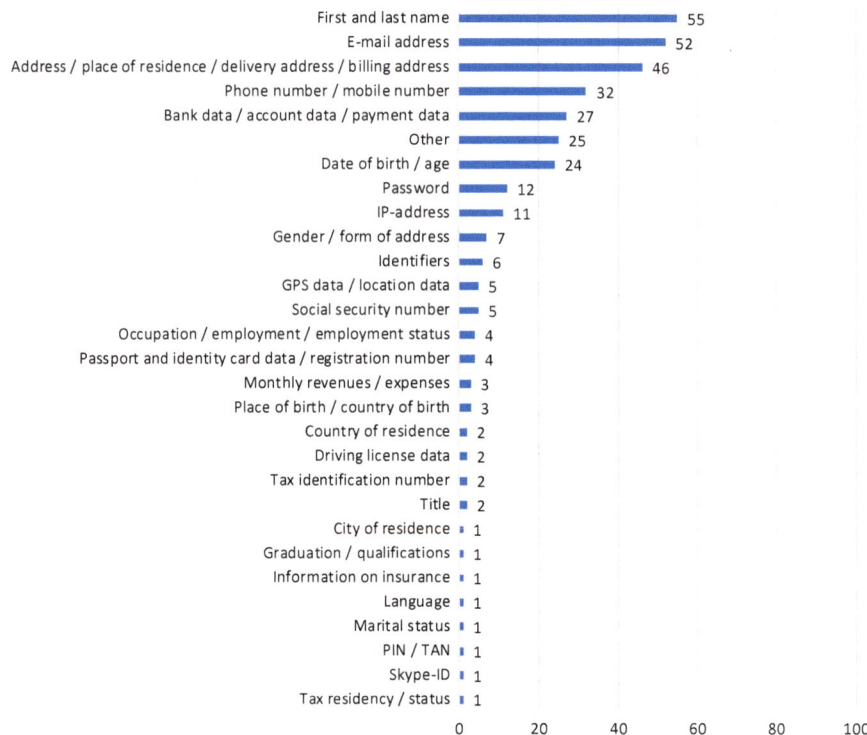

Fig. 3.9 Types of personal data processed according to the privacy statement in the payment segment. Number of evaluated privacy statements $N = 104$

In addition to personal data, as of September 2009, the BDSG defined in § 3 special categories of personal data as "*information on racial or ethnic origin, political opinions, religious or philosophical beliefs, trade-union membership, health or sex life*" (translation by the authors). The GDPR includes a similar definition in Article 9. The Regulation states: "*Processing of personal data revealing racial or ethnic origin, political opinions, religious or philosophical beliefs, or trade union membership, and the processing of genetic data, biometric data for the purpose of uniquely identifying a natural person, data concerning health or data concerning a natural person's sex life or sexual orientation shall be prohibited.*" According to the privacy statements of the FinTech companies, some of these data were processed before the GDPR became binding. After the commencement of the GDPR, processing of these data is still possible as long as users explicitly provide consent to it.

FinTechs in the segment financing often noted processing data about the nationality of users. This serves the purpose of organizing the financing or preparing the annual fiscal certificate for investors. FinTechs in the financing segment often stated

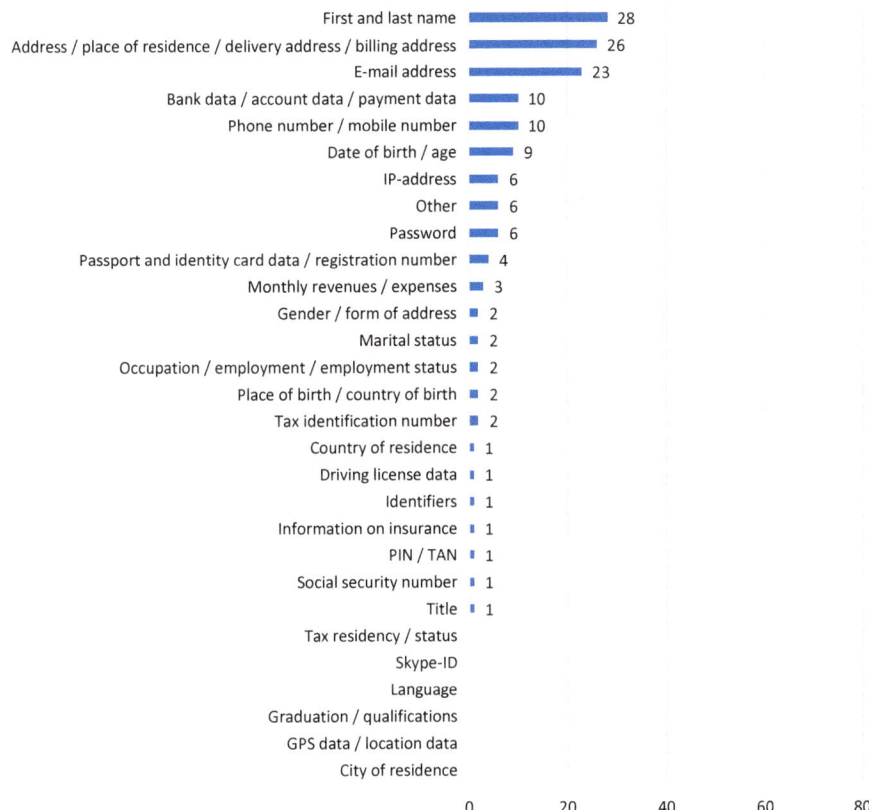

Fig. 3.10 Types of personal data processed according to the privacy statement in the asset management segment. Number of evaluated privacy statements $N = 80$

that they process pictures of users if the users uploaded a profile picture or video to promote or support financing.[4] The personal financial management provider Numbrs, for example, offers users an identification via fingerprint and facial recognition. Other FinTech companies stated that they use specimen signatures for authentication. Furthermore, FinTechs in the insurance segment and the personal financial management provider feelix process health-related data.[5] To identify users,

---

[4]For example, the privacy statement of Numbrs stated (originally in German, translation by the authors): "During the process of video identity verification, pictures and video recordings are made to compare the user data on the identity document with the user data processed during the application process. Furthermore, the audio of the conversation is recorded."

[5]The insurance manager Clark, for example, noted that (originally in German, translation by the authors): "Peculiarities regarding health-related data: Particular insurances require the disclosure of health-related data (e.g., health or life insurance). As health-related data are particularly important, we therefore ask for your explicit approval to collect and process this type of data. We shall only use this data if necessary to support you or to carry out your orders such as taking out new insurance.

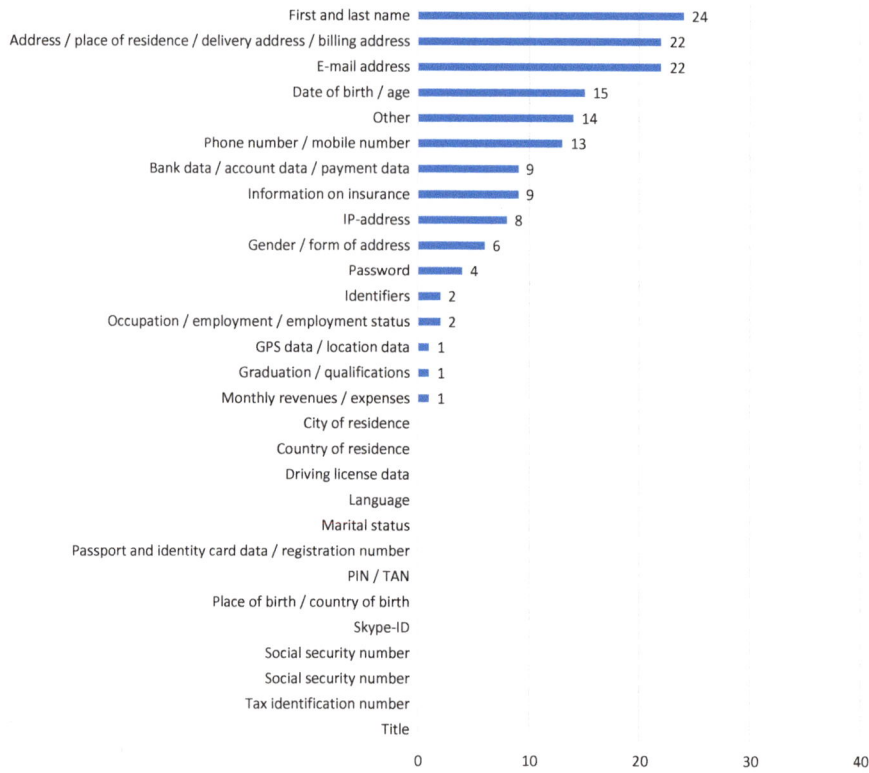

Fig. 3.11 Types of personal data processed according to the privacy statement in the insurance segment. Number of evaluated privacy statements $N = 41$

FinTechs in the payment segment mentioned recording conversations. PayPal and BTC Express explicitly stated that they process these types of data. The equity crowdfunding provider Unternehmerich also mentioned processing data related to religious background. Figures 3.13, 3.14, 3.15, 3.16, 3.17, and 3.18 provide an overview of the usage of special categories of personal data in the particular FinTech segments.

According to the GDPR, an enterprise is "*a natural or legal person engaged in an economic activity, irrespective of its legal form, including partnerships or associations regularly engaged in an economic activity.*" Company data are not personal data and, therefore, are not subject to the BDSG or the GDPR. However, FinTechs processed various data related to particular companies. As Fig. 3.19 shows, they most often processed data related to the company name, the address, the business form, and the register number.

We only share your data if you have explicitly and separately agreed to it. You can revoke the respective approval anytime."

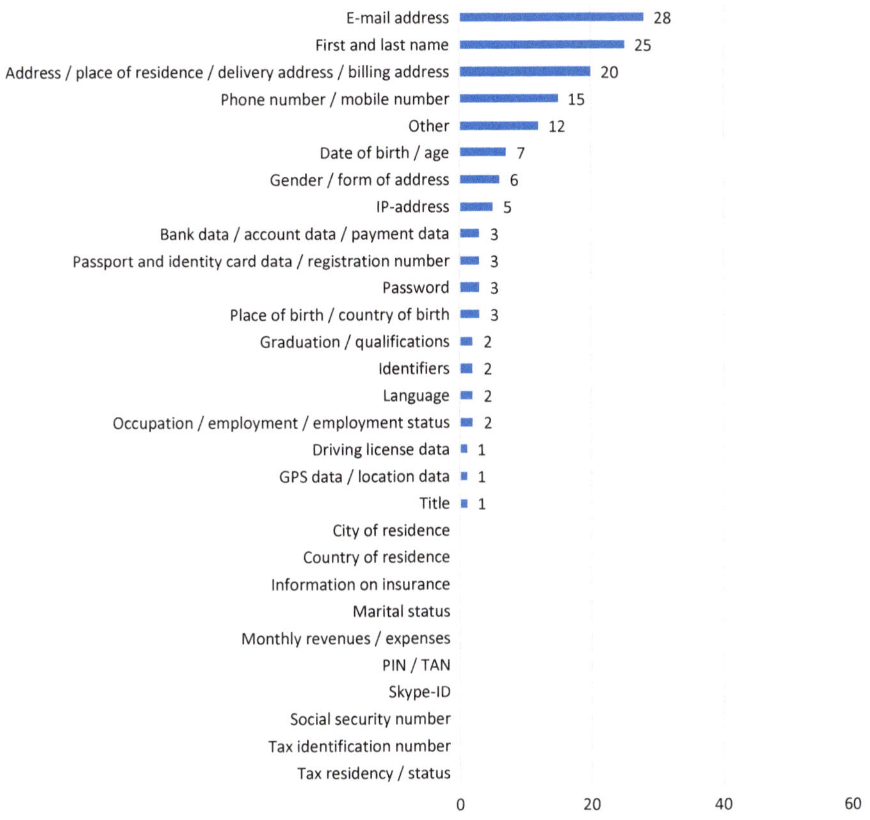

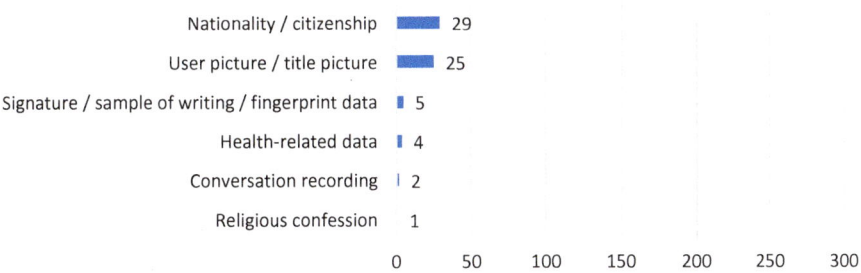

Fig. 3.12 Types of personal data processed according to the privacy statement in the other FinTechs segment. Number of evaluated privacy statements $N = 60$

Nationality / citizenship	29
User picture / title picture	25
Signature / sample of writing / fingerprint data	5
Health-related data	4
Conversation recording	2
Religious confession	1

Fig. 3.13 Special categories of personal data processed according to the privacy statement. Number of evaluated privacy statements $N = 375$

Only recently has the European Court of Justice clarified in a judgment of 19.10.2016 (C-582/14) that IP addresses are considered data that could be related to individuals and thus are personal data. Figure 3.20 shows that 85% ($N = 321$) of

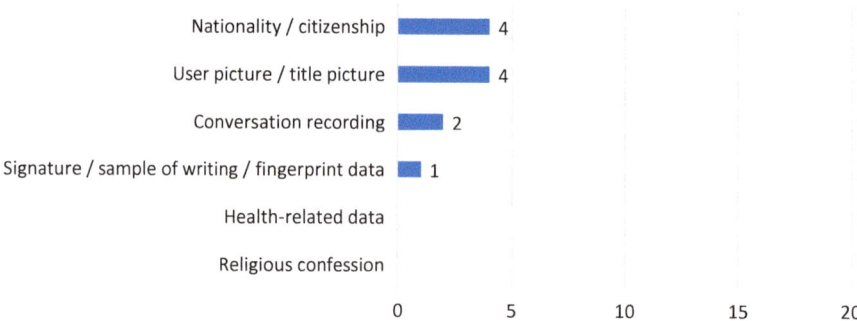

Fig. 3.14 Special categories of personal data processed according to the privacy statement in the payment segment

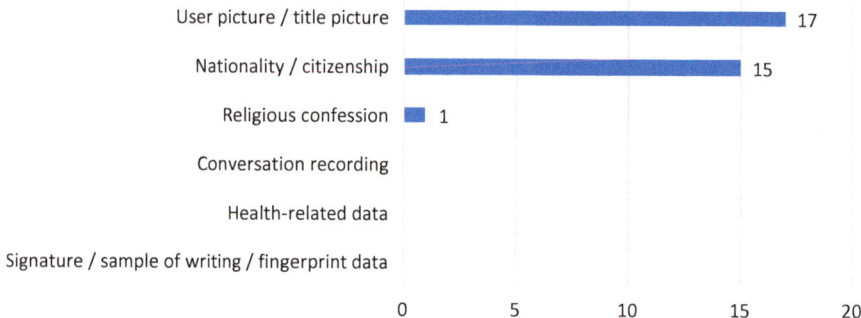

Fig. 3.15 Special categories of personal data processed according to the privacy statement in the financing segment

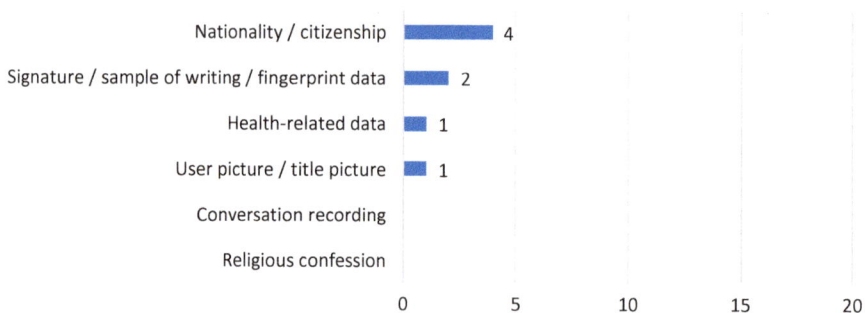

Fig. 3.16 Special categories of personal data processed according to the privacy statement in the asset management segment

FinTechs mentioned processing users' IP addresses. The remaining FinTechs did not specify in their privacy statement whether they process IP addresses or not. The majority of the FinTechs processed the IP address to make use of web-tracking

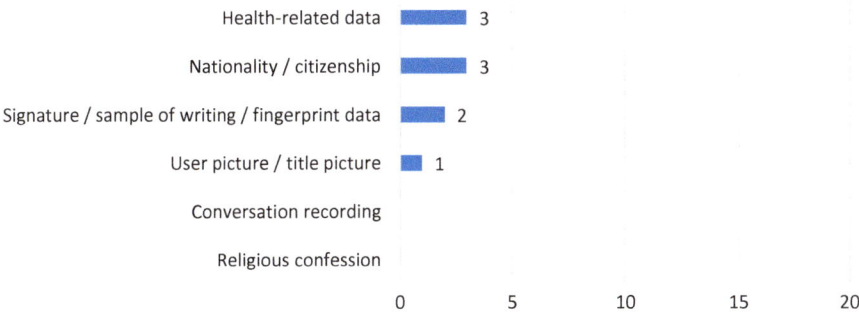

Fig. 3.17 Special categories of personal data processed according to the privacy statement in the insurance segment

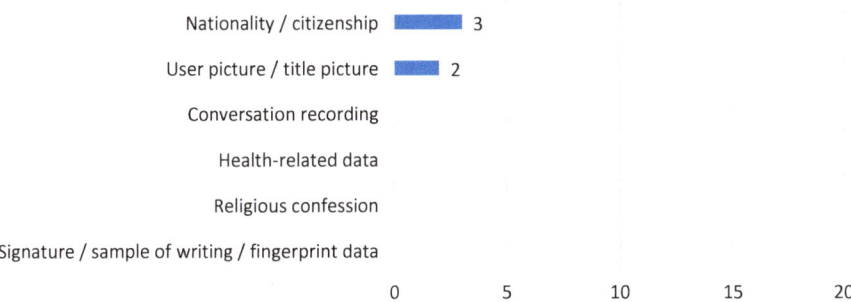

Fig. 3.18 Special categories of personal data processed according to the privacy statement in the other FinTechs segment

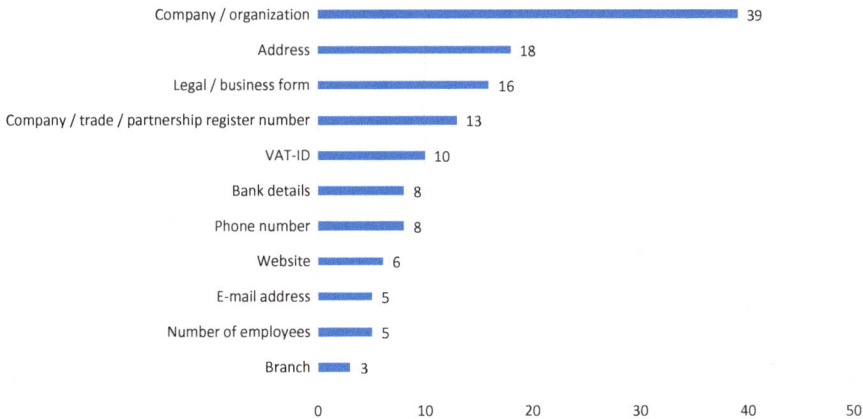

Fig. 3.19 Type of company-related data processed according to the privacy statement. Number of evaluated privacy statements $N = 375$

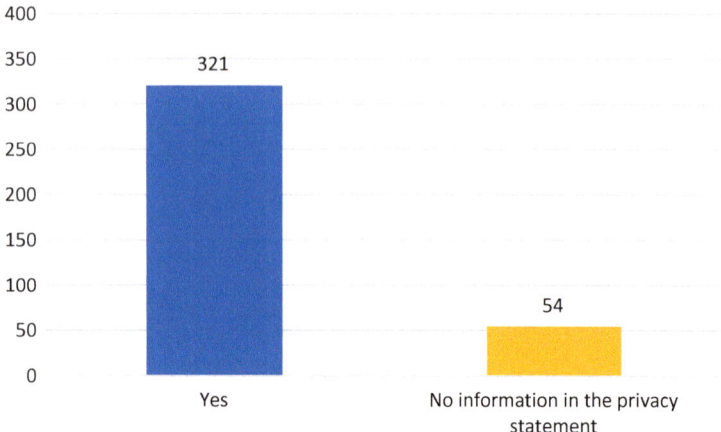

Fig. 3.20 Is the IP address processed abridged or unabridged? Or does a third-party process the IP address? Number of evaluated privacy statements $N = 375$

services (83%, $N = 291$) and social plug-ins (30%, $N = 105$). Additional reasons were for the usage of advertising services, newsletters, and features such as blogs, chats, and video conferences.[6] Often, FinTechs argued that processing IP addresses is important for "the security of the company" or "the interest of the user" or mentioned the necessity to share data with law enforcement.[7] Other privacy statements did not specify any reasons for processing IP addresses. Figure 3.21 presents the purposes of processing users' IP addresses. The bars in dark blue indicate that the IP addresses are processed unabridged.

Most of the privacy statements not only stated a reason for storing the IP addresses but also mentioned reasons for processing personal data. Figure 3.22 shows that 84% ($N = 316$) of the FinTech companies justified the processing of personal data in their privacy statements. Most often, FinTechs stated that the processing of data is necessary for contractual purposes and the service delivery for users. This could include the simple contacting of users. The second most

---

[6]For example, the privacy statement of AnyoneCan states (originally in German, translation by the authors): "I send e-mails about blog posts and/or e-mails containing information about my services and offers only in explicit consent with the user. Users can revoke the consent to the newsletter anytime. Therefore, the possibility to revoke is, among other, included in each e-mail. I have to record the registration to properly proof it. Therefore, I store the time of registration, the time of confirmation, and the IP address of the respective user."

[7]For example, the privacy statement of Econeers states (originally in German, translation by the authors): "To ensure an effective access protection, Econeers may temporarily store your IP address. IP addresses are sequences of numbers that serve the addressing of data packages online. In cases of a report of misuse, the IP address of the complaint pseudonymous will be stored one time at the first login after the report of misuse, and as soon as there is a respective court order, we share the IP address as well as other personal data with responsible law enforcement. If the report of misuse turns out to be unfounded we delete the stored IP address immediately."

Fig. 3.21 In which context are the IP addresses of the users processed? Number of evaluated privacy statements $N = 375$

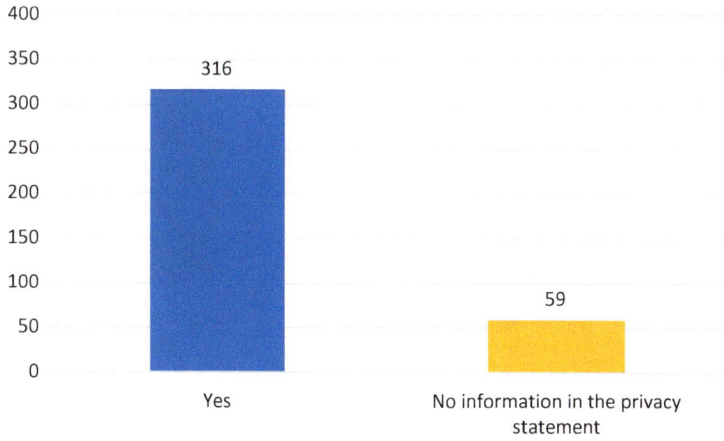

Fig. 3.22 Is a reason given for processing personal data? Number of evaluated privacy statements $N = 375$

common reason for the processing of personal data was for marketing, self-promotion, third-party advertising, and the sending of newsletters (72%, $N = 227$). Of significantly less importance was customer security and the fulfillment of legal provisions (18%, $N = 56$), as well as the creation of user profiles to improve

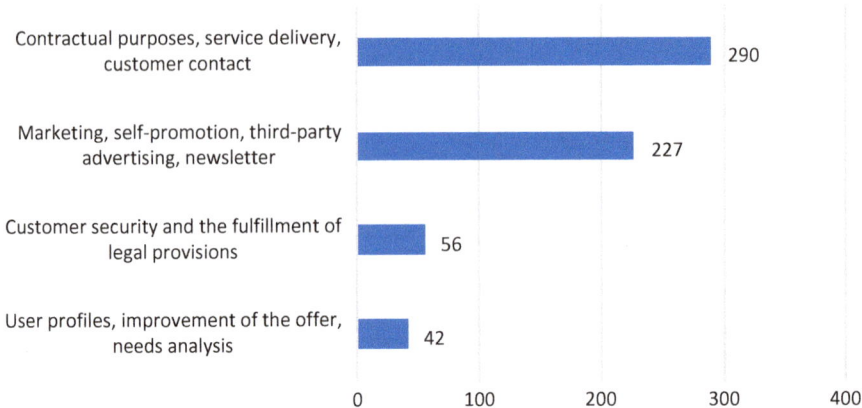

Fig. 3.23 Which reason is given for processing personal data? Number of evaluated privacy statements $N = 375$

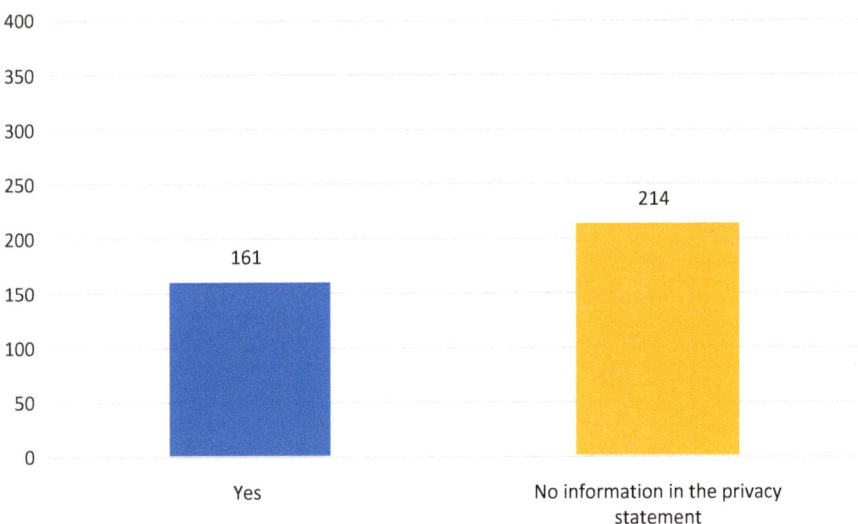

Fig. 3.24 Is it specified how long data are stored or when data are deleted? Number of evaluated privacy statements $N = 375$

offers (13%, $N = 42$). Figure 3.23 provides an overview of the mentioned reasons for the collection of personal data.

According to Article 15 Sec. 1 GDPR, users have the right to obtain information about the planned period for which their personal data will be stored or, at least, the criteria used to determine that period. As Fig. 3.24 shows, with a share of 43% ($N = 161$), not even half the FinTech companies stated how long they will store users' personal data.

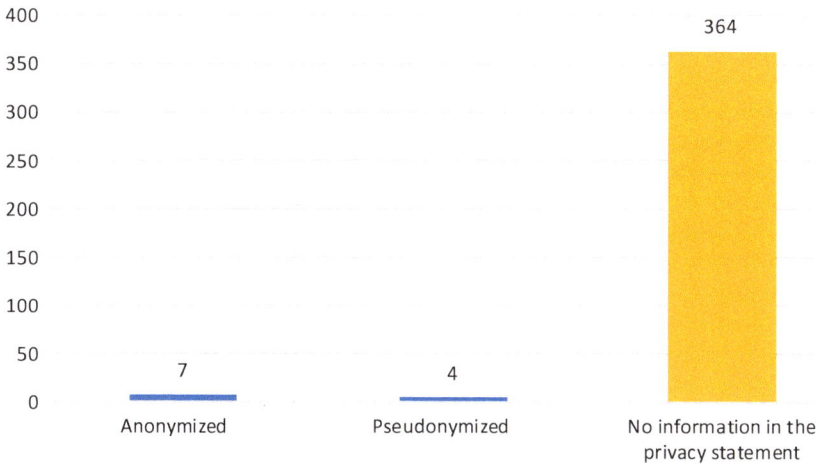

Fig. 3.25 Are data processed anonymously or pseudonymously? Number of evaluated privacy statements $N = 375$

If reference to a specific person within the processed data is not allowed, pseudonymization can be used. This procedure eliminates the immediate disclosure of a user during data processing. If, for example, an on-screen blocking (pixelating) of a profile picture can be redone later on, the data keep the reference to users. If the consideration of further information does not lead to a clear association between the data and a natural person, the data are anonymized. We analyzed the privacy statements of the FinTechs regarding whether they use pseudonymization or anonymization in their data processing.

In general, the mentioning of pseudonymization or anonymization was extremely rare, and as Fig. 3.25 shows, only 11 privacy statements included a respective note. In particular, FinTechs in the segments donation- and reward-based crowdfunding, equity crowdfunding, and crowdlending used anonymization. The FinTechs often used special user accounts to anonymize the user data. Moreover, the personal financial management provider finatra allowed users to obtain a personal financial analysis anonymously with a guest account. To pseudonymize the user data, FinTechs used special user accounts as well. Notably, the pseudonymization was not usually the default solution but needed to be selected by the user (opt-in solution).

Furthermore, we analyze whether the FinTechs published personal data according to their privacy statements. The results are shown in Fig. 3.26. For example, a crowdfunding platform published personal data if the profile pictures of the users were publicly visible on the website.

In total, 14% ($N = 53$) of the FinTech companies that provided a privacy statement mentioned that they publish personal data. The remaining 86% ($N = 322$) did not include respective information in the privacy statement. Comparatively often, FinTechs in the segments crowdlending (46%, $N = 7$) and donation-

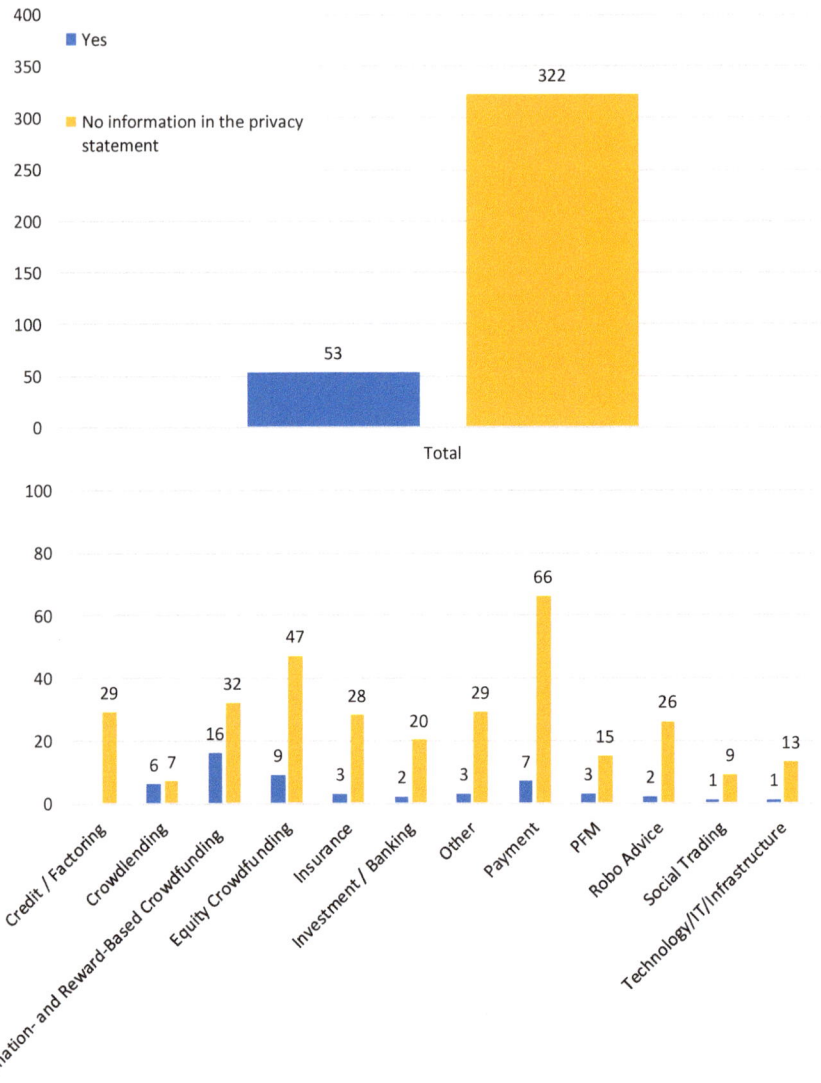

Fig. 3.26 Are personal data published? Distinction by FinTech Segment, $N = 375$

and reward-based crowdfunding (33%, $N = 16$) published personal data. The FinTechs stated that the publication of personal data was necessary for a public or nonpublic user profile (68%, $N = 36$), for comments or blog function (25%, $N = 13$), or for other reasons (8%, $N = 4$). Figure 3.27 presents the frequency of the mentioned reasons for the publication of personal data.

With a share of 83% ($N = 310$), the great majority of FinTech companies mentioned not only processing the personal data of users but also sharing the data

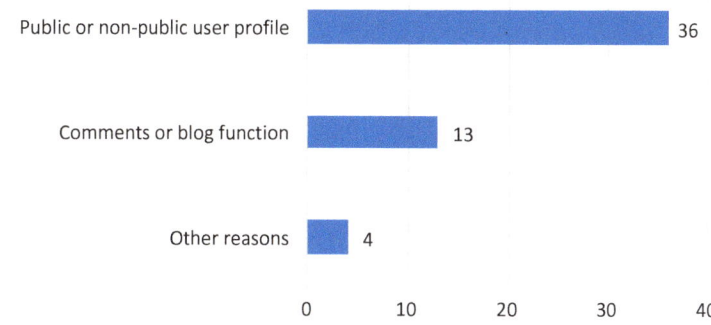

Fig. 3.27 For what reason are personal data published? Number of evaluated privacy statements $N = 375$

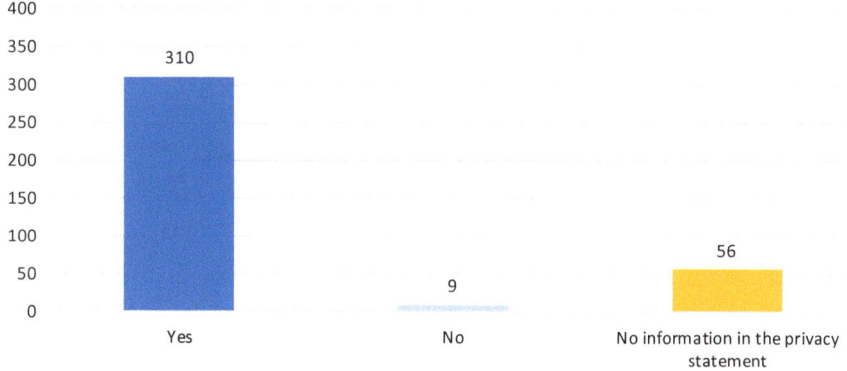

Fig. 3.28 Are personal data shared with third parties with consent? Number of evaluated privacy statements $N = 375$

with third parties. As Fig. 3.28 shows, only 2% ($N = 9$) of the FinTechs stated that they do not share the data with third parties. For 15% ($N = 56$) of the FinTechs, we were not able to identify whether they shared the data with third parties by analyzing the privacy statements.

As Fig. 3.29 shows, only a few of the FinTechs listed in their privacy statement what types of personal data of users they share with third parties. Only 10% ($N = 37$) of the FinTech companies provided a specific list describing those with whom they shared the data. In total, 8% ($N = 30$) at least gave examples of the personal data they shared. However, as Fig. 3.29 highlights, most privacy statements did not clarify what personal data are shared, even though they mentioned the sharing of data with third parties.

Figure 3.30 shows what data were shared with third parties. Often, the FinTechs shared information about the name, the address, the e-mail address, or data regarding the bank, the account, and payment data of the users. The latter information was

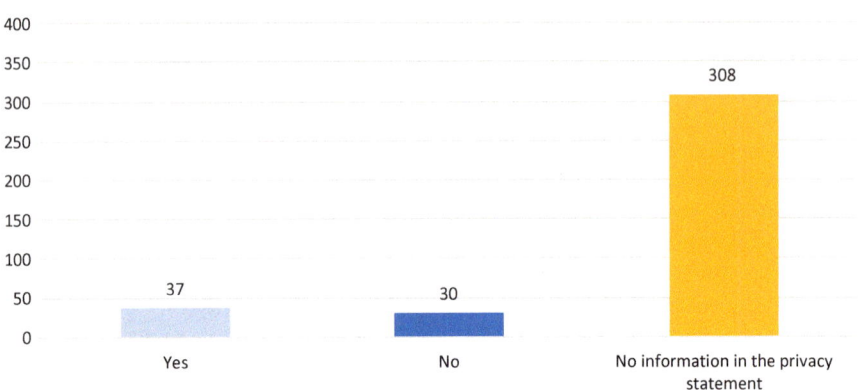

Fig. 3.29 Is there an exhaustive statement on what personal data are shared with third parties? Number of evaluated privacy statements $N = 375$

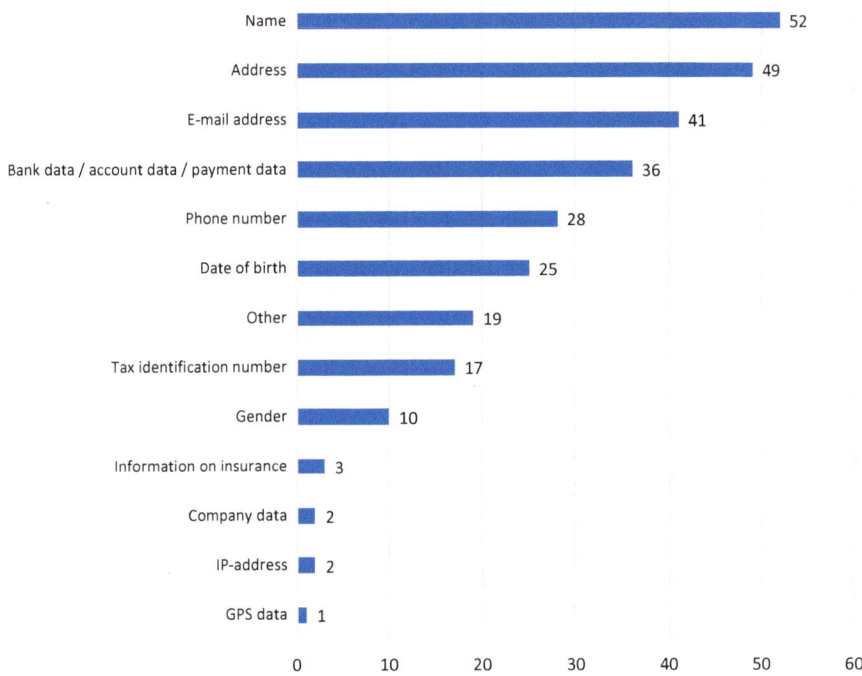

Fig. 3.30 What personal data are shared with third parties? Number of evaluated privacy statements $N = 375$

particularly shared by FinTechs in the equity crowdfunding segment. According to the information provided by the FinTech companies, data transfer took place primarily for the purpose of fulfilling the contract, processing orders, and providing services or out of obligations arising from the user relationship (41%, $N = 126$) and for processing payments or other transactions (e.g., accounting, payment of instalments, granting of a loan, and support of account transactions) (28%, $N = 88$). The third most frequent reason mentioned was for advertising, marketing, and the dispatch of newsletters (10%, $N = 32$). Figure 3.31 gives an overview of the reasons for the disclosure of personal data mentioned in the data protection statements.

Article 4 GDPR defines a third party as "*a natural or legal person, public authority, agency or body other than the data subject, controller, processor and persons who, under the direct authority of the controller or processor, are authorised to process personal data.*" However, it is questionable whether users' data were shared exclusively because this was necessary for the execution of a transaction or whether the passing on of the data belonged to the FinTech business model and was remunerated by third parties. Information about whom the user data will be shared with could help answer this question. Figure 3.32 shows that just under half (48%, $N = 179$) of the privacy statements revealed to whom the user data was shared. Even more rarely (18%, $N = 69$), the privacy statements included an exhaustive list of who the third parties receiving the data were. Often the list was not exhaustive (30%, $N = 111$) or the FinTech companies stated, as Fig. 3.33 shows, that users' personal data are passed on to third parties "only in exceptional cases."

Some privacy statements also indicated that personal data are not only shared with third parties but also collected by the FinTech companies from third parties and linked to the data of their own users. Figure 3.34 shows that only a few FinTechs explicitly named the third parties (10%, $N = 37$). These were Bürgel Wirtschaftsinformationen GmbH & Co. KG, Schufa Holding AG, and Creditreform Boniversum GmbH.

As Fig. 3.35 shows, half the FinTech companies (50%, $N = 187$) stated in their privacy statements that they used so-called social plug-ins. These functions, which are offered by third parties, help disseminate the content of the users or the FinTech company. For example, Facebook's social plug-in with a "Like" button and Twitter's social plug-in with a "Tweet" button allow users to share the content on the company website of the FinTech on social networks. Information is transmitted from the browser of the user to Facebook and other third parties. The FinTech companies usually mentioned in their privacy statements that they have no influence on the transmission and no knowledge of the use of these data. Rather, they referred to the privacy statement of the respective third party for questions about the type, purpose, and scope of the data collected and their processing and use. Figure 3.36 lists the companies whose social plug-ins were used by FinTech companies. Almost half stated in their privacy statement that they used a social plug-in from Facebook (48%, $N = 180$). The social plug-ins from Twitter (33%, $N = 122$) and Google+ (26%, $N = 97$) were also particularly popular. Social plug-ins from LinkedIn, Xing, YouTube, Vimeo, Instagram, and Pinterest were less frequently included (less than 10% each).

Almost all FinTech companies (96%, $N = 360$) stated in their privacy statement that they use web tracking services to collect and evaluate data on the behavior of users on their website. Web tracking enables FinTech companies to track which Internet sites users visit before or at the same time, which content they call up on the

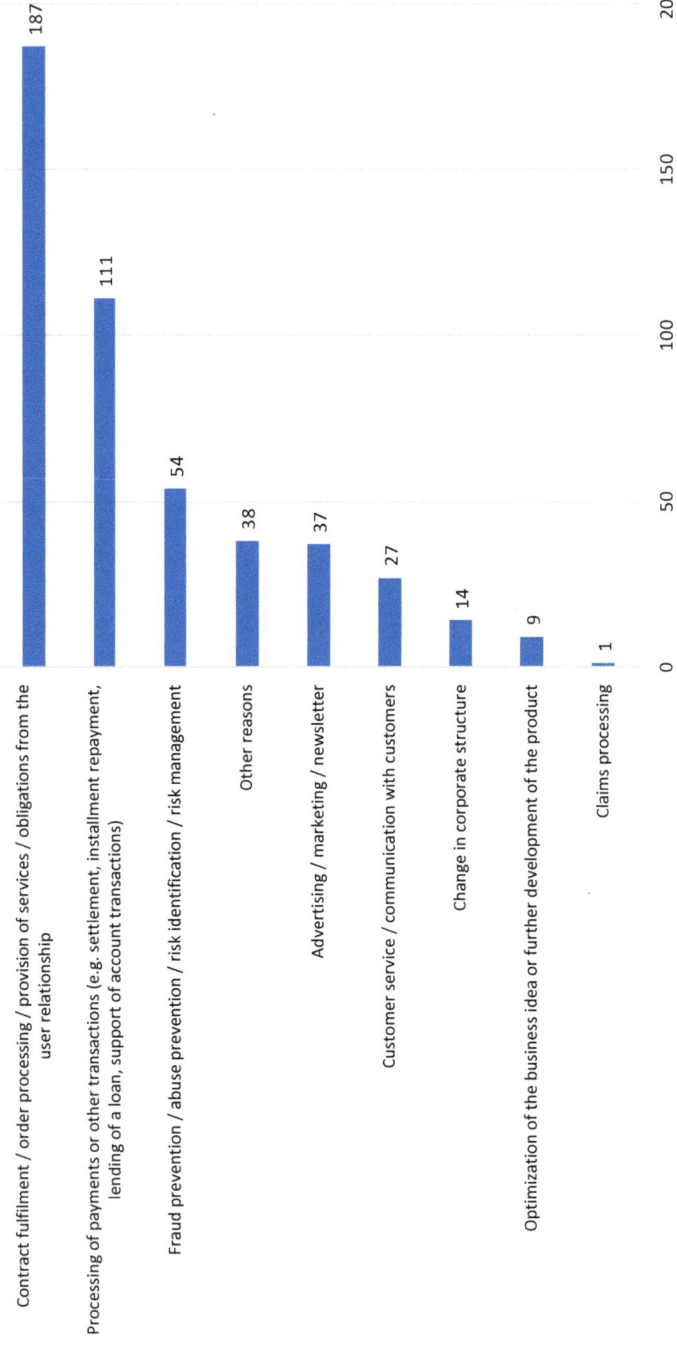

Fig. 3.31 For what purpose are personal data shared with third parties? Number of evaluated privacy statements $N = 375$

Fig. 3.32 Is it indicated to which third parties data are shared? Number of evaluated privacy statements $N = 375$

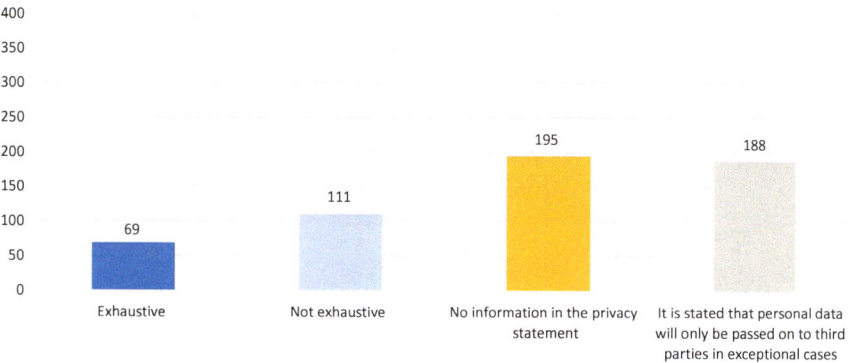

Fig. 3.33 Is there an exhaustive or nonexhaustive indication to which third parties' data are transmitted? Number of evaluated privacy statements $N = 375$

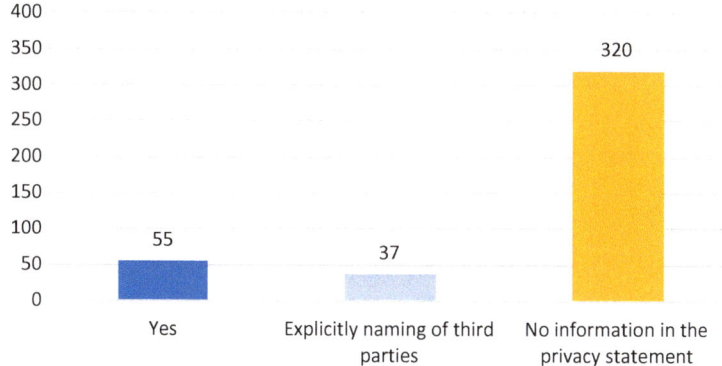

Fig. 3.34 Are personal data collected from third parties? Number of evaluated privacy statements $N = 375$

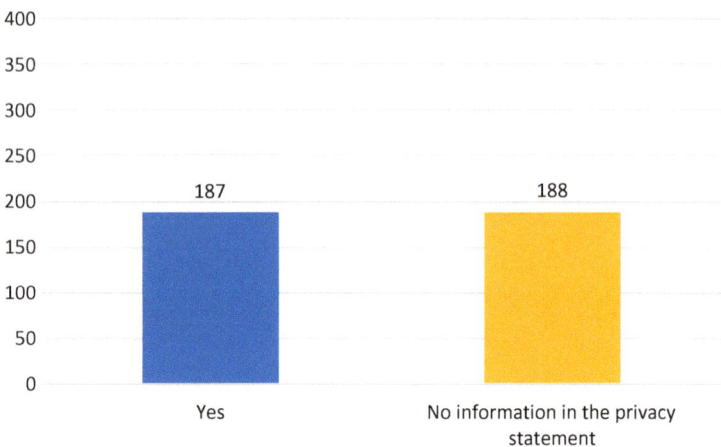

Fig. 3.35 Does the company's website use social plug-ins or are third-party services integrated? Number of evaluated privacy statements $N = 375$

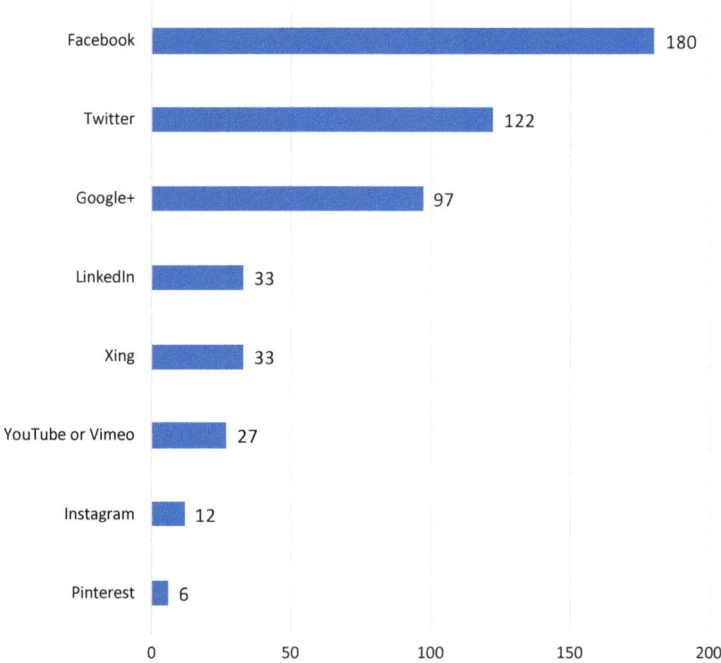

Fig. 3.36 Which third-party social plug-ins or services use FinTech companies? Number of evaluated privacy statements $N = 375$

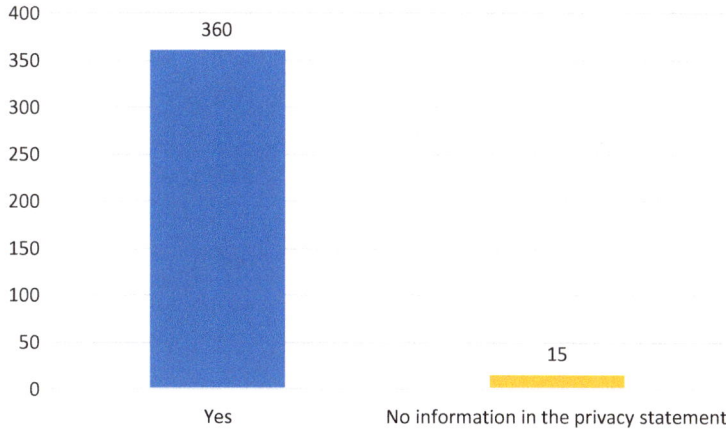

Fig. 3.37 Are behavioral, usage, or movement data processed or are tracking services used? Number of evaluated privacy statements $N = 375$

website, how often and for how long they view this content, and where they subsequently migrate to. In addition to anonymized and pseudonymized data, the majority of web tracking services process personal user data (Bundesamt für Sicherheit in der Informationstechnik 2014). Figure 3.37 shows how frequently FinTech companies used web tracking services. The privacy statements included 75 different web tracking services. Three of four FinTech companies use Google Analytics (76%, $N = 285$). As Fig. 3.38 shows, some FinTechs used up to 11 different web tracking services. Figure 3.39 shows other services listed by at least three FinTech companies in their privacy statements. Other frequently used services are Piwik, Hotjar, Optimizely, Mouseflow, and etracker.

Somewhat less relevant than the tracking services were advertising services such as Google AdSense or Google AdWords. These services enable FinTechs to, for example, display advertising on web pages outside their own pages. Google AdSense uses an algorithm that takes into account the content of the target web page on which the ad is placed. AdWords personalizes advertising based on search queries on the Google search engine. The different services and additional programs of Google, Facebook, LinkedIn, and Twitter were grouped together in one category each. Some FinTech companies were unable to correctly name the specific services of the third-party providers and wrote, for example, "Google Remarketing" or "Google Conversion Tracking," both of which are part of Google AdWords.

We identified 22 advertising services in the privacy statements. More than one-quarter of the FinTechs used Google advertising services (28%, $N = 104$). Figure 3.40 shows that more than one-third of the third-party software used by FinTech is for advertising purposes. As Fig. 3.41 shows, some FinTechs used up to eight different advertising services. Figure 3.42 lists other advertising services mentioned by at least three FinTech companies in their privacy statements. Of the

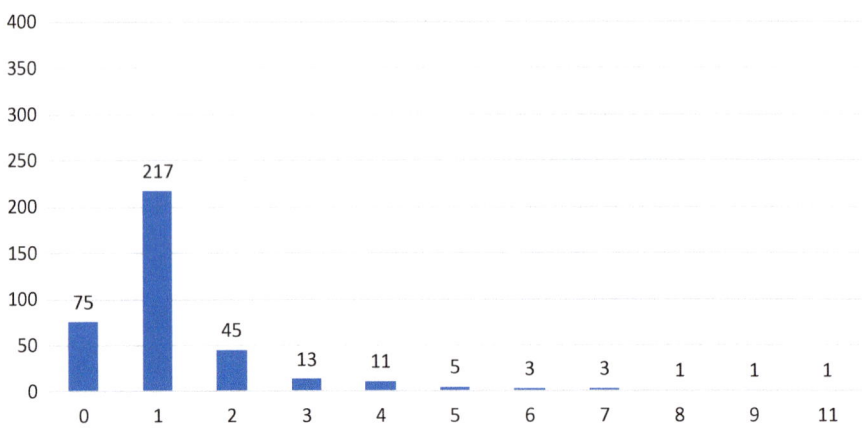

Fig. 3.38 Number of web tracking services used by FinTech companies. Number of evaluated privacy statements $N = 375$

services, Google, Facebook, Bing Ads, LinkedIn, Outbrain, and Twitter were frequently used.

If we add the tracking and advertising services used together, as shown in Fig. 3.43, up to 19 different services were sometimes used by the FinTechs. Figure 3.44 also gives an overview of the frequency of services used in the different FinTech segments. It is clear that no FinTech segment has a particularly right-skewed distribution and therefore that the frequency with which these services were used is not segment specific.

The purpose of cookies is often to store information associated with a website locally on the computer of the user for a certain period and then to transmit this information back to the server of the FinTech company on request.[8] Cookies allow a website to be individualized for the user by authenticating the user when he or she returns to the respective web page. Just over three-quarters of FinTechs reported using cookies (see Fig. 3.45). The remaining FinTech companies did not provide any information on the use of cookies. In 31% of the cases ($N = 89$), the FinTech companies stated that they store cookies permanently. In total, 37% of the FinTechs ($N = 105$) mentioned only using temporary cookies. In the remaining privacy statements, the FinTechs provided no statement about the type of cookies used. However, many companies used both temporary and permanent cookies.

Finally, data were also transmitted to the FinTech companies via the browser or the end device used by the users through so-called server log files. In this context, more than one-third of the FinTech companies provided an exhaustive list of the data

---

[8]When cookies are used, questions often arise about the storage location of the data processed. For example, an excerpt from the privacy statement of the company 360T states (originally in German, translation by the authors): "The information generated by the cookie about the use of this website by visitors is generally transferred to a Google server in the USA and stored there."

Fig. 3.39 Frequency of web tracking services used by FinTech companies. Number of evaluated privacy statements $N = 375$

processed (38%, $N = 141$). Another 29% ($N = 107$) at least drew up a nonexhaustive list. For 34% ($N = 126$) of the FinTechs, we did not find any information about the server log files. Figure 3.46 shows the data processed using log files. Figure 3.47 gives an overview of how often a list of what data were transmitted through server log files was specified in the privacy statements, either exhaustively or not exhaustively.

Although the privacy statements by the FinTech companies provided a direct and immediate overview of the processing of users' personal data, this analysis is subject to certain limits in terms of content, especially if the FinTech companies provided certain information incompletely or not at all. For this reason, we conducted interviews with some FinTech experts also on the subject of data protection.

Figure 3.48 shows the answers to the question of what data protection risks would arise from FinTechs (question 7 in Appendix A.2). Many of the respondents stressed that there were no FinTech-specific risks (13 mentions). It was often emphasized that FinTechs, which are relatively young companies, had systematically organized their

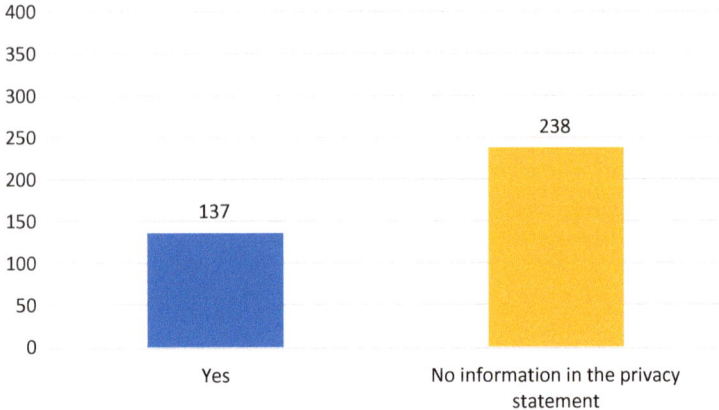

Fig. 3.40 Is third-party software used for promotional purposes? Number of evaluated privacy statements $N = 375$

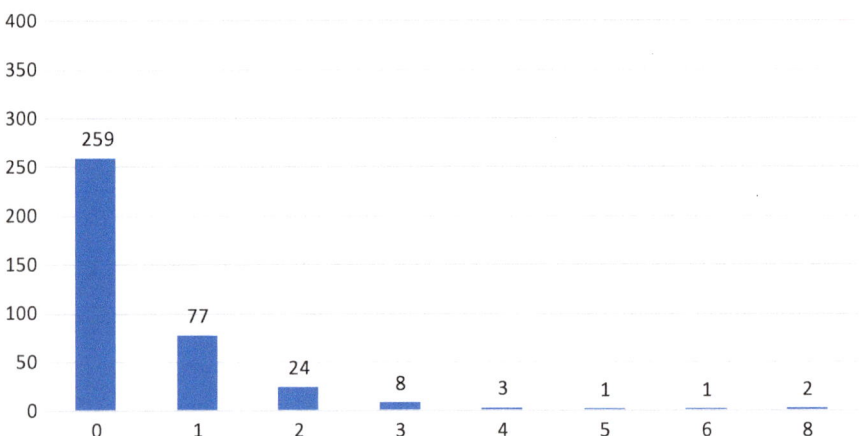

Fig. 3.41 Number of advertising services used by FinTech companies. Number of evaluated privacy statements $N = 375$

IT processes and also professionally implemented data protection. However, this view was not shared by all respondents who, in turn, explicitly mentioned the following risks:

- *Data security/data theft*: In particular, the mobile devices the customers used created risks (e.g., near-field communication might not be secure). In addition, concrete real cases of data theft were mentioned (e.g., Equinix in the USA).
- *Data misuse*: FinTechs as start-up companies process a great deal of data because, if not, they would have little capital. The principles of data economy would not be followed. Because start-ups or FinTechs do not have a customer base, they are inclined to process general data, most of which are public. The Internet was

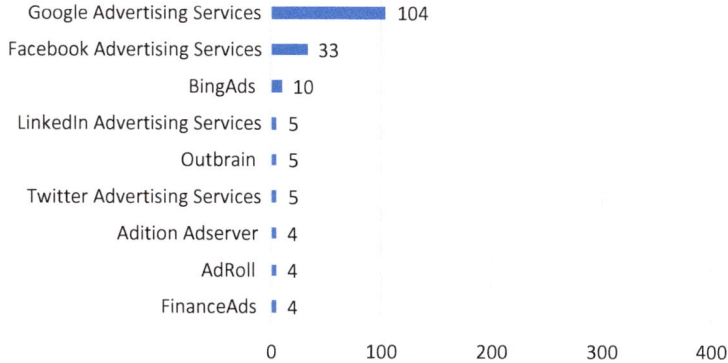

Fig. 3.42 Frequency of advertising services used by FinTech companies. Number of evaluated privacy statements $N = 375$

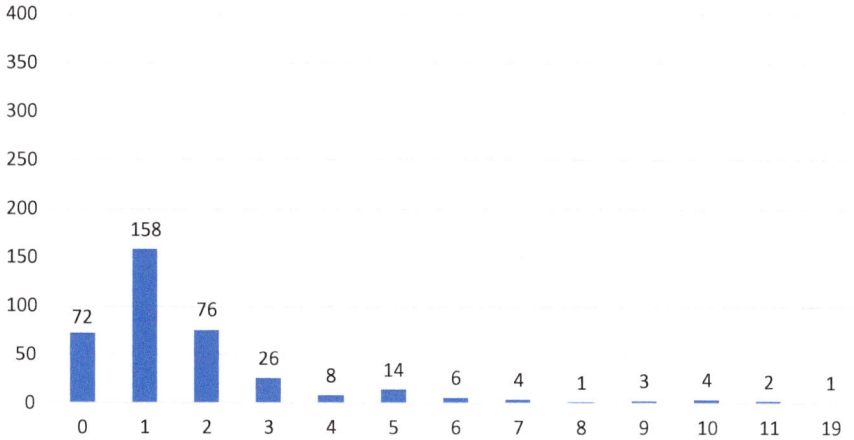

Fig. 3.43 Number of web tracking and advertising services used by FinTech companies. Number of evaluated privacy statements $N = 375$

regarded as a general source of data, but it is not. In the case of start-ups, it was also apparent that the owners changed quickly, and this created uncertainty about the use of data. Furthermore, not every FinTech was highly professional in data processing and anonymization. The sale of data shortly before insolvency was a risk especially for start-ups (four mentions). Certain risks might be deliberately accepted by FinTechs, but they would have too little capital to be liable for the risks.

- *Data sales*: Five of the experts mentioned the risk that FinTechs would resell their customers' data. Although this might be covered by the privacy statement accepted by the customers, such a sale could still happen against their will, as many do not read the statements.

Fig. 3.44 Number of web tracking and advertising services used by FinTech companies by FinTech segment. Number of evaluated privacy statements $N = 375$

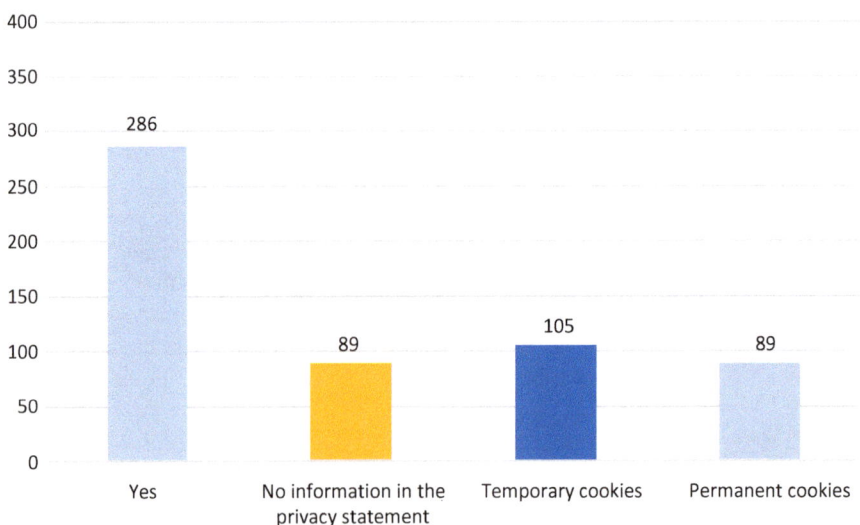

Fig. 3.45 Does the FinTech company provide information on the use of cookies? Number of evaluated privacy statements $N = 375$

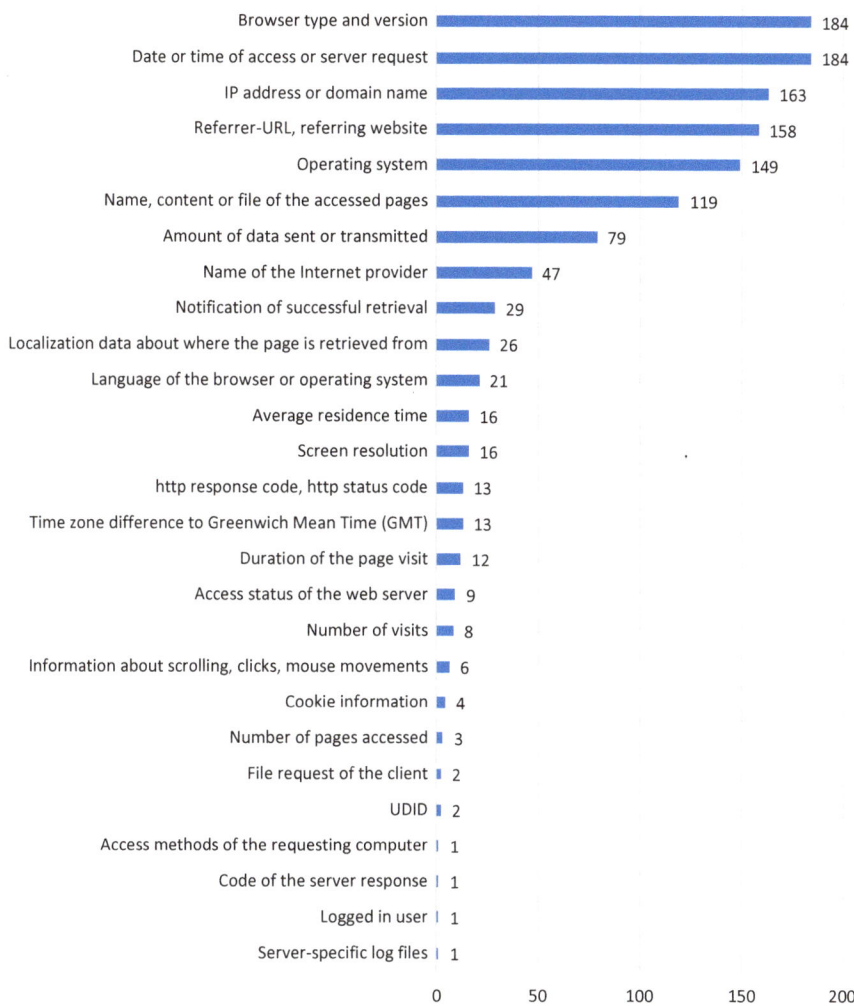

Fig. 3.46 Frequency of data processed by log files. Number of evaluated privacy statements $N = 375$

The experts mentioned other aspects as well:

- FinTechs often demand more data from customers than are necessary for a particular transaction, thereby ensuring more freedom for the FinTech company. The sensitivity of customers to their data is often overestimated. Three experts believed that the majority of users did not read the privacy statements or read them only superficially.
- There is a difference between FinTechs and banks when it comes to data protection risks. Banks in Germany do not use cloud solutions but operate their

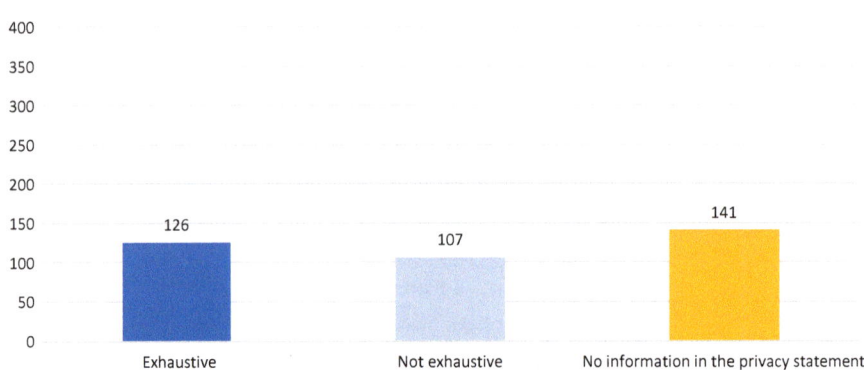

Fig. 3.47 Frequency with which the privacy statements provide an exhaustive or nonexhaustive list of what data are transmitted through server log files. Number of evaluated privacy statements $N = 375$

own data centers, backups, and redundant systems. FinTechs often do not do this and use services such as Amazon Simple Storage Service (S3) more frequently.

- Penalties for data protection infringements are turnover-related and therefore are more relevant for banks than for FinTechs.
- There is an equal legal framework for all market participants, especially when FinTechs have reached a certain size.
- Depending on the technology and the specific business model of the FinTech, a different accentuation of the risks can result. For example, the Second Payment Services Directive established a direct link to the GDPR and thus directly instructed payment service providers to comply with certain data protection requirements.
- The elimination of intermediaries has led to a bundling of competencies and data. More data are also generated, more easily increasing the risk. However, there are no more risks to data protection and data security because they are FinTechs. The reasons for the higher risks are the changed technological basis and business models.

In summary, the experts stressed that the crucial factors in this question are what data would be processed, where the data would actually be stored (on a cloud server or in-house), and how the data would be protected. Furthermore, the respondents stated that it was important how strictly the existing regulations were being followed by FinTechs and checked and enforced by the supervisory authorities. In addition, they noted that it was important whether the customer had the possibility to waive the respective financial service. The model in which customers agreed to the use of their data does not offer a solution to this problem, because even with a selection of a different provider, there can be no alternative to the data processed by the provider.

We also asked the experts about the implementation of data protection by FinTechs (question 8 in Appendix A.2). The answers are shown in Fig. 3.49.

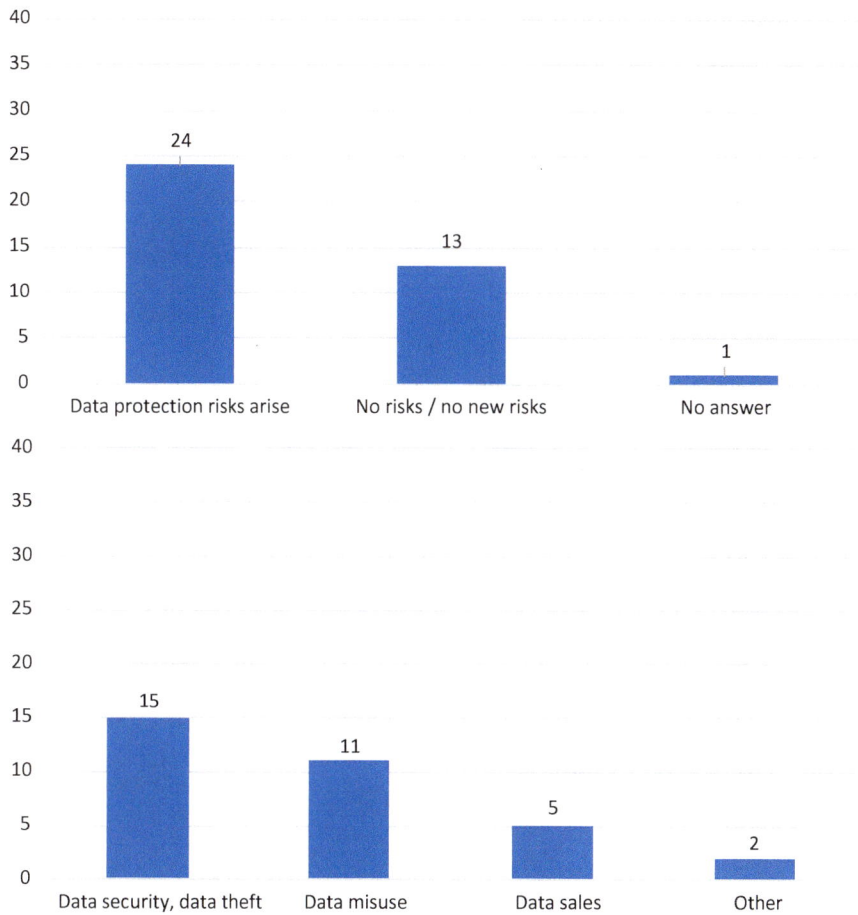

Fig. 3.48 Answers to the question of privacy risks by FinTechs. The upper graph shows the answers to the question whether privacy risks exist, while the lower graph shows which ones these are (multiple answers possible)

Initially, seven respondents were unwilling or unable to talk about this question. With regard to the other answers, we divided them into three categories *ex post*.

- *Minimalistic implementation*: The respondents noted that many FinTechs as start-ups had little data protection capacity and/or regarded data protection as an obstacle to their business model. A further argument mentioned here was that the in-house lawyers at larger FinTechs were "the [people] for everything" and had to have very broad knowledge. One respondent stated that Anglo-American FinTechs often only perceived a lawyer as a disturbing factor.
- *Very good implementation*: 12 respondents said that FinTechs implemented data protection very well. The following statements were made in this regard:

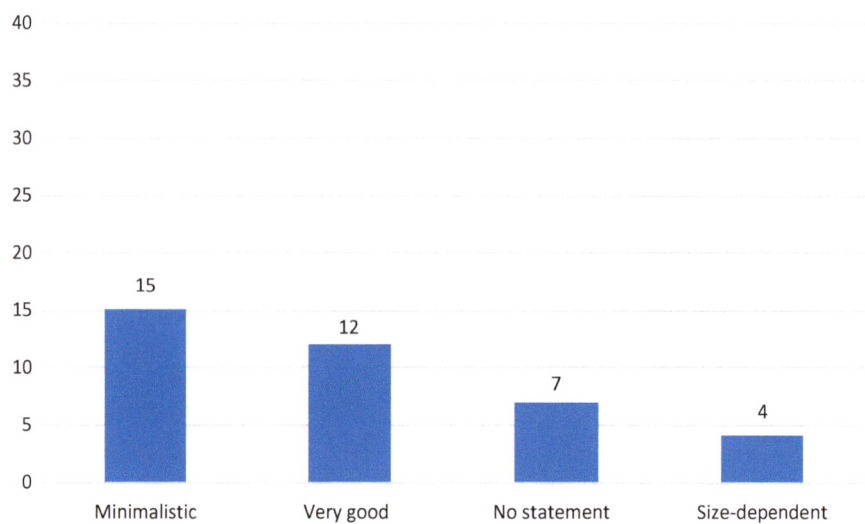

Fig. 3.49 Answers to the question about the implementation of data protection at FinTechs

- MaRisk (the minimum requirements for risk management published by BaFin) should be applied. In this context, there will be no difference between banks and FinTechs.
- Established FinTechs often have an internal and/or external data protection officer.
- There are inspections and discussions by data protection authorities.
- Security audits by customers take place. Some FinTechs are voluntarily certified by the TÜV.
- Processes are implemented to determine who is allowed to access certain data and processes. In addition, creating a leaner data structure than banks is a great opportunity for FinTechs.

- *Size-dependent implementation*: Seven of the respondents essentially expressed the opinion that FinTechs implement data protection depending on their size. While small FinTechs have little time and capacity to do so, the privacy efforts of larger and more established FinTechs are comparable to those of a bank.

Moreover, the experts explicitly mentioned the following measures on how FinTechs implement data protection:

- The FinTechs create certain functions relevant to data protection. A compliance officer will sometimes exist, even if he or she only performs this function once a week. In general, data protection-relevant functions are often performed by the CEO or other executives (one mention).
- FinTechs often have no certification for the establishment, implementation, maintenance, and continuous improvement of an information security management system in accordance with ISO/IEC 27001 but are on their way there or

outsource these services using Infrastructure as a Service (IaaS), Platform as a Service (PaaS), or Software as a Service (SaaS) via cloud computing.

Additional aspects listed by the individual experts are as follows:

- Some employees no longer needed in other departments are often transferred to the compliance department at major banks. The compliance department is therefore often not staffed with the most qualified employees.
- Some FinTechs refrain from using US servers for storing data in the meantime.
- Some FinTechs have abolished the web-based instant messaging service Slack as a communication tool within workgroups for privacy reasons.
- Some FinTechs use nudges to implement data protection. For example, in a certain FinTech, employees need to bring a cake if they did not activate a blocking screen while they were not at work.

The third question on the subject of data protection was whether banks indeed have a trust bonus over FinTechs with regard to protecting customers' data (question 9 in Appendix A.2). Figure 3.50 shows the answers. Almost all respondents agreed on the existence of a trust bonus (33 mentions). Some experts mentioned that it is a generational issue of whether customers put more trust in banks (six mentions). This was the case for older people more than younger people. However, the respondents stressed that it was only a matter of time before this would change (two mentions). Three respondents explicitly noted, however, that this trust bonus was not objectively justified.

Analysis of the privacy statements of the FinTech companies operating in Germany in 2017 shows that the provision of information on the processing of personal data to users had the potential for improvement in many respects. As noted previously, in every fourth FinTech company, even after intensive research we could not find a privacy statement that provided information about what personal data were processed and to whom they were shared. Particularly obscure was the information about what data were processed when third-party services (e.g., social plug-ins) were integrated. This lack of information left a great deal of uncertainty as to what personal data the respective FinTech company were actually processing. The expert interviews also suggested that the partly nontransparent and nonexhaustive provision of information could be a conscious strategy of some companies to request certain data from users to create more freedom for possible future business models. Such a strategy violates the principle of data economy and data reduction.

The strategy of requesting more data than are necessary for a particular transaction also reflects a general trend of start-up companies in systematically crossing regulatory boundaries to trigger certain regulatory changes. When users become accustomed to the services and like using them, many also become political advocates for reforming the law in the interests of the respective company. Pollman and Barry (2017) introduce the term "regulatory entrepreneurship" in this context. In addition, Rohleder (2015) reports that at least in 2015, more than 60% of users of online services did not read the respective privacy statements or only read them superficially and approximately 80% agreed to the statements without understanding

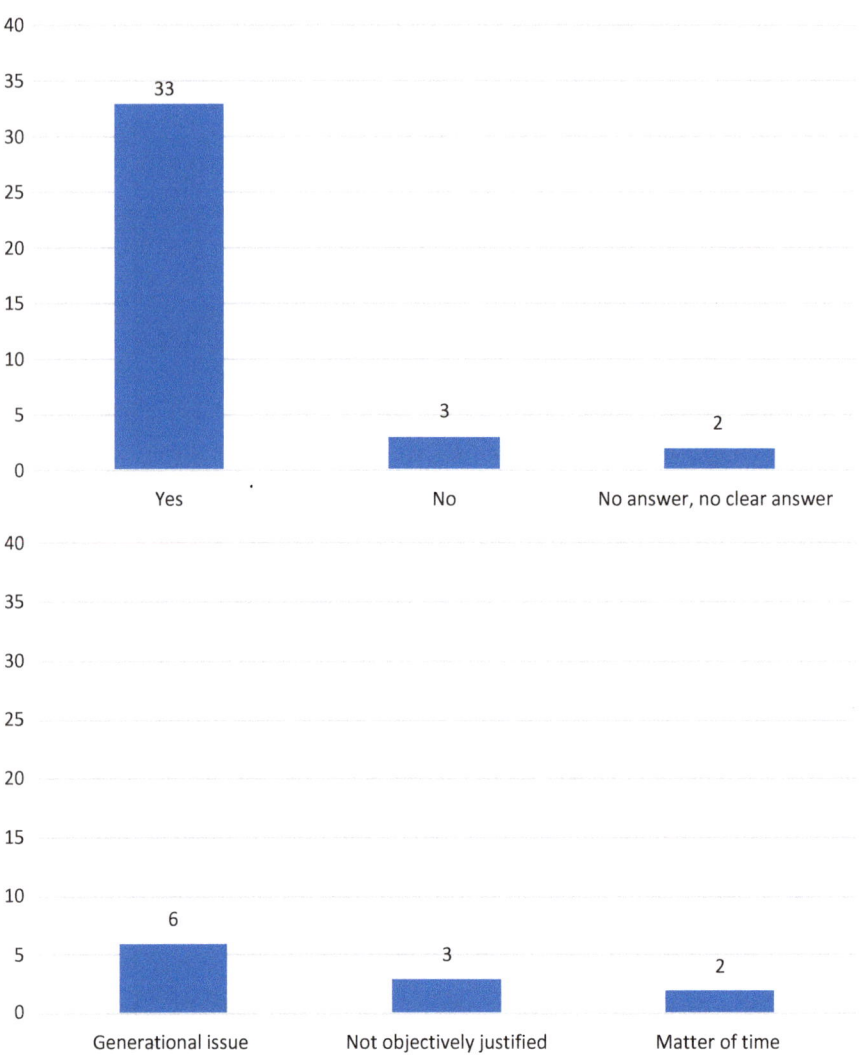

Fig. 3.50 Answers to the question of a bank's trust bonus. The upper panel shows the answers to the question whether banks enjoy a trust bonus over FinTechs with regard to data protection; the lower panel shows differentiation of the yes answers (multiple answers possible)

them. However, as we have shown, some FinTech companies did provide comprehensive and exhaustive information about the data processed and endeavored to implement appropriate data protections. According to the experts interviewed in our study, younger generations are also undergoing a shift, putting more trust in FinTech companies than in traditional banks. According to a survey of 1007 consumers by the industry association Bitkom (2016), more than two-thirds put their trust in an Internet portal for financial matters, while only one in three puts trust in a bank adviser. According to the Bankenverband (2017), however, only 3% of Germans would shift their banking business to TechFins such as Amazon.com, Facebook, or Google.

References

Bankenverband (2017). *Peters: Banken punkten bei Datensicherheit.* Retrieved from https://bankenverband.de/newsroom/presse-infos/peters-banken-punkten-bei-datensicherheit/
Bitkom (2016). *Verbraucher vertrauen in Finanzfragen auf Online-Portale.* Retrieved from https://www.bitkom.org/Presse/Presseinformation/Verbraucher-vertrauen-in-Finanzfragen-auf-Online-Portale.html
Bundesamt für Sicherheit in der Informationstechnik (2014). *M 2.488 Web-Tracking.* Retrieved from https://www.bsi.bund.de/DE/Themen/ITGrundschutz/ITGrundschutzKataloge/Inhalt/_content/m/m02/m02488.html
Dorfleitner, G., Hornuf, L., Schmitt, M., & Weber, M. (2019). Marktüberblick. In F. Möslein & S. Omlor (Eds.), *FinTech-Handbuch. Digitalisierung, Recht, Finanzen* (pp. 21–38). Munich: C.H.Beck.
McDonald, A. M., & Cranor, L. F. (2009). The cost of reading privacy policies. *I/S: A Journal of Law and Policy for the Information Society, 4*(3), 543–568.
Pollman, E., & Barry, J. M. (2017). Regulatory entrepreneurship. *Southern California Law Review, 90*, 383–448.
Rohleder, B. (2015). *Datenschutz in der digitalen Welt.* Retrieved from https://www.bitkom.org/Presse/Anhaenge-an-PIs/2015/09-September/Bitkom-Charts-PK-Datenschutz-22092015-final.pdf

Chapter 4
FinTechs and Data Protection After the Implementation of the GDPR

Abstract This chapter deals with data protection regarding FinTech services and how FinTechs dealt with it after the implementation of the GDPR in May 2018. The primary source of information on how FinTechs are handling data protection is the privacy statements of the respective companies. We analyzed these privacy statements with regard to three questions: What user data are processed? To whom are these data forwarded? And, if applicable, which third parties provide further information?

This chapter deals with data protection in FinTech services after the GDPR became binding and forms the main part of this book. As in Chap. 3, we use the privacy statements of the respective FinTechs as data sources for analysis. To examine changes in the period before and after the GDPR became binding, we again collected the privacy statements of all 505 German FinTech companies in the period from August 15, 2018, to October 31, 2018, and examined what user data are processed, with whom these data are shared, and from which third parties' information is obtained.

Since May 25, 2018, the GDPR has been directly applicable in all EU member states, including Germany. Besides the GDPR, the new BDSG became binding on May 25, 2018. In addition to a general section, this act includes provisions related to the GDPR and the implementation of the European Directive on the protection of individuals with regard to the processing of their personal data by competent authorities for the purposes of prevention, investigation, detection, and prosecution of criminal offences or the execution of sentences, as well as on the free movement of data and the repeal of the Council Framework Decision 2008/977/JHA (Directive 2016/680). Changes in the content of privacy statements may, therefore, be due to general trends in the design of the privacy statements, the changes in the GDPR, and the implementation of the Directive.

Of the 505 FinTechs analyzed by Dorfleitner et al. (2019), 65 did not have a website in the period from October 15, 2017, to December 20, 2017, and, accordingly, no online privacy statement. In the period from August 15, 2018, to October 31, 2018, 94 FinTechs did not have a website. In 2017, 65 FinTechs had a website, but even after intensive research, we could not find a privacy statement. After the

© Springer Nature Switzerland AG 2019

G. Dorfleitner, L. Hornuf, *FinTech and Data Privacy in Germany*,

https://doi.org/10.1007/978-3-030-31335-7_4

GDPR became biding, 41 FinTechs had an Internet site, but no privacy statement. We found a separate or integrated privacy statement on the websites of 370 companies. When we examined the individual FinTech segments (see Fig. 4.1), all FinTechs in the segment of loans and factoring ($N = 29$) now provided a privacy statement. However, privacy statements were still rare in the segments personal financial management (53%, $N = 16$), donation- and reward-based crowdfunding (63%, $N = 46$), and equity crowdfunding (67%, $N = 50$).

On average, privacy statements in 2018 with a length of approximately eleven A4 pages (min.: <1 page; max.: 37 pages) and 4183 words (min.: 20 words; max.: 16,899 words) are now more than twice as long as in 2017. Assuming a reading speed of 250 words per minute, the average reading time of a privacy statement is just over 17 min. In extreme cases, users will need more than 1 h to read the privacy statement in full. In the period after the GDPR became binding, privacy statements increasingly use standardized text modules, while in the period before, individualized text was still frequently added. The standardization of the privacy statements has not, in general, contributed to a noticeable improvement in readability.

Moreover, many companies state that the processing of personal data is based on the GDPR, though some FinTechs highlight that the processing of personal data is based on a right of access that is not German law. As Fig. 4.2 shows, Swiss law has become particularly popular. All other rights, especially English law, lost in popularity. Companies that do not explicitly refer to European or foreign law continue to refer to German law.

At 98% ($N = 363$), the absolute majority of FinTech companies continue to report that they process personal data. Again, none of the FinTech companies explicitly state that no personal data are processed. At 2% ($N = 7$), companies still provide no information on the type of data processed in their privacy statements. Figure 4.3 shows the breakdown of segments in which no information is provided about the type of data processed.

Reexamination of the privacy statements confirms that information about the types of personal data provided is not exhaustively listed in the majority of cases. The proportion of FinTechs that exhaustively list the data processed even fell from 38% ($N = 143$) to 28% ($N = 102$). Instead, examples of personal data are now cited more frequently, though it is not clear whether these data are actually processed. The phrases "for example," "possibly," and "among other things" are still used. As Fig. 4.4 shows, instead of 56% ($N = 209$) in 2017, 71% ($N = 261$) now provide a nonexhaustive list of processed personal data. In only 2% ($N = 7$) of the privacy statements is there still no indication what personal data are processed at all. The crowdlending (38%, $N = 5$) and insurance (34%, $N = 10$) segments continue to provide indications of the processed personal data. The processed personal data in the technology, IT, and infrastructure segment are the least frequently named.

After examining whether the FinTech companies had exhaustively or nonexhaustively stated what personal data were processed, in a second step we analyzed why no conclusive list could be found in 261 privacy statements. Figure 4.5 shows that significantly more FinTech companies (70%, $N = 184$) now only cite examples of what personal data are processed. We found 23% more specific

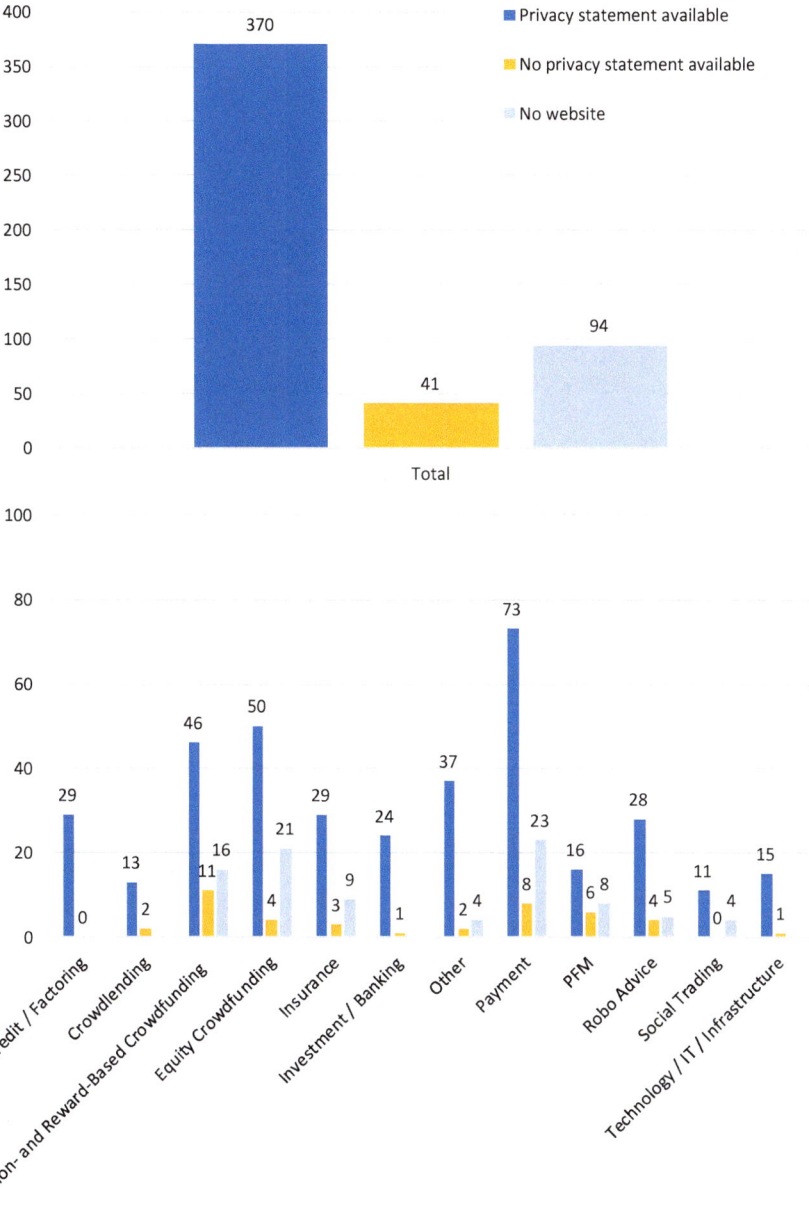

Fig. 4.1 Frequency of providing a privacy statement after the implementation of the GDPR. Distinction by FinTech Segment. Number of evaluated privacy statements $N = 505$

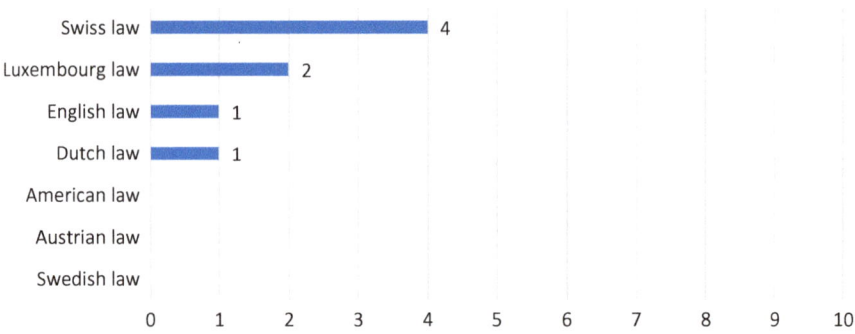

Fig. 4.2 Law applicable to data processing if a foreign law was explicitly mentioned after the implementation of the GDPR. Number of evaluated privacy statements $N = 370$

individual mentions of personal data in the privacy statements in 2018 than in 2017. In some cases, data categories are provided in which examples of specific personal data are listed. Here, it is usually not clear from the privacy statements whether and what data from the categories are actually processed or which individual entries only serve as examples.[1] In total, 20% ($N = 51$) of FinTech companies refer to a legal definition[2] of what personal data are, but now slightly fewer companies (10%, $N = 26$) only state that such data are processed. The provision of examples is particularly common in the subsegments social trading and crowdlending. A legal definition often appears in the privacy statements from the subsegment technology, IT, and infrastructure. Reference to the collection of personal data also frequently appears in the data protection statements of the technology, IT, and infrastructure subsegment.

In the following examination, we analyze the data listed in the privacy statements, whether conclusive or not, that are processed by the FinTech companies according to their privacy statements. In most cases, data such as e-mail address (77%, $N = 285$), name (74%, $N = 275$), address (55%, $N = 205$), and telephone number (46%, $N = 172$) continue to be processed. Now also listed are IP addresses (34%, $N = 125$), the collection category other (31%, $N = 113$), information on the age of

---

[1]For example, the privacy statement of Appsichern states (originally in German, translation by the authors): "Types of data processed: inventory data (e.g., names, addresses), contact data (e.g., e-mail, telephone numbers), content data (e.g., text input, photographs, videos), usage data (e.g., websites visited, interest in content, access times), and meta/communication data (e.g., device information, IP addresses). Categories of persons concerned: visitors and users of the online service (hereinafter referred to collectively as 'users')."

[2]A frequently used text module in the privacy statements is "Personal data is any information relating to an identified or identifiable natural person (hereinafter 'data subject'). A natural person shall be considered identifiable if he or she can be identified directly or indirectly, in particular by reference to an identifier such as a name, an identification number, location data, online identifier or to one or more specific characteristics expressing the physical, physiological, genetic, psychological, economic, cultural or social identity of that natural person" (originally in German, translation by the authors).

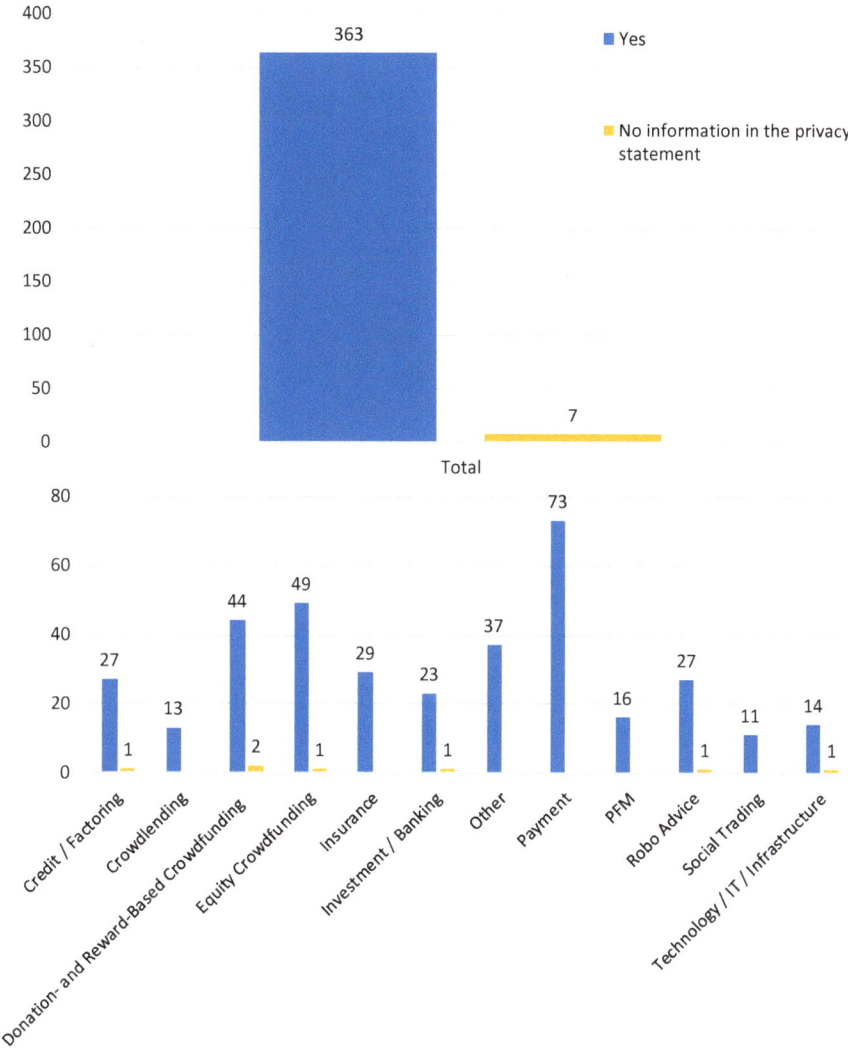

Fig. 4.3 Frequency of privacy statements indicating that personal or personally identifiable information is being processed after the implementation of the GDPR. Distinction by FinTech Segment. Number of evaluated privacy statements $N = 370$

users (30%, $N = 109$), account and payment data (28%, $N = 105$), and passwords (19%, $N = 69$). Figure 4.6 shows the breakdown of data categories for the entire FinTech market. Moreover, 42 instead of 25 FinTechs state that they process passports or ID cards and their registration numbers, 23 state that they process information on the occupational or employment situation, and 10 state that they

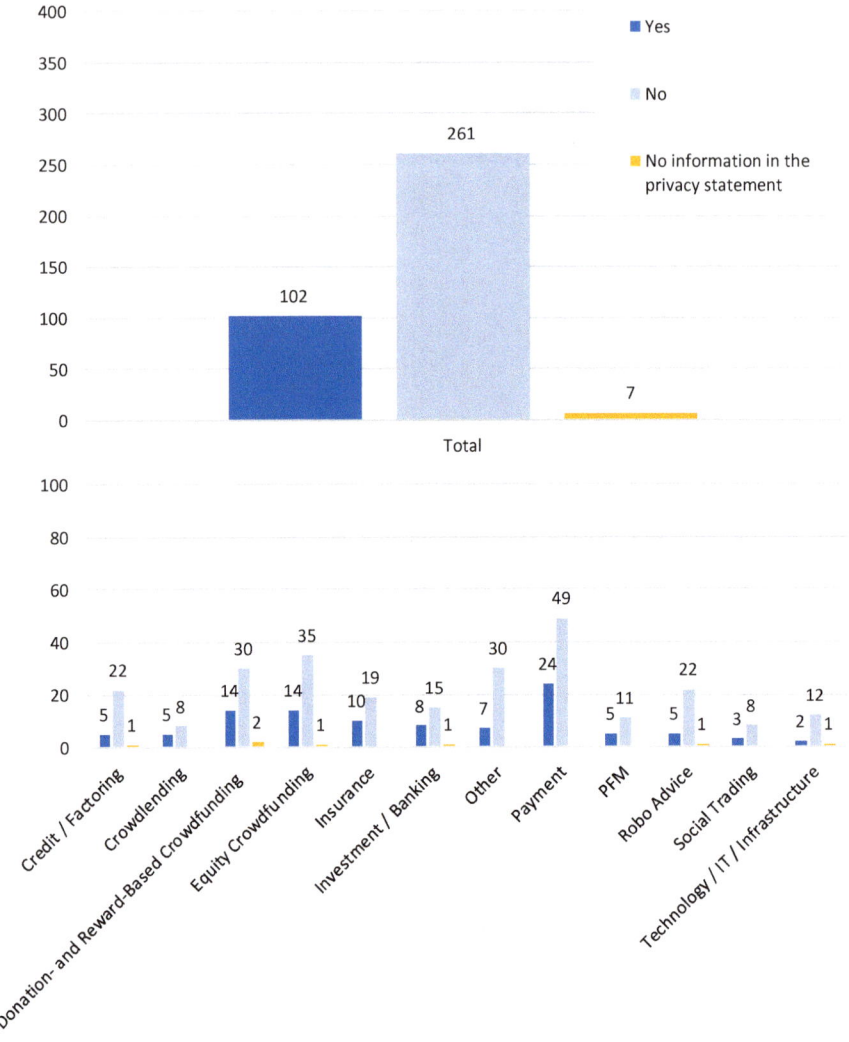

Fig. 4.4 Frequency of privacy statements reporting what personal data are processed after the implementation of the GDPR. Distinction by FinTech Segment. Number of evaluated privacy statements $N = 370$

process GPS and location data. Overall, all types of data are now being mentioned more frequently in the data protection statements.

Figure 4.7 shows that FinTechs are now more likely to process personal data in a business context. In particular, the processing of data on the position of a person in a company is frequently referred to explicitly. In general, however, this category continues to be mentioned rather rarely, with 13 mentions, and therefore is not

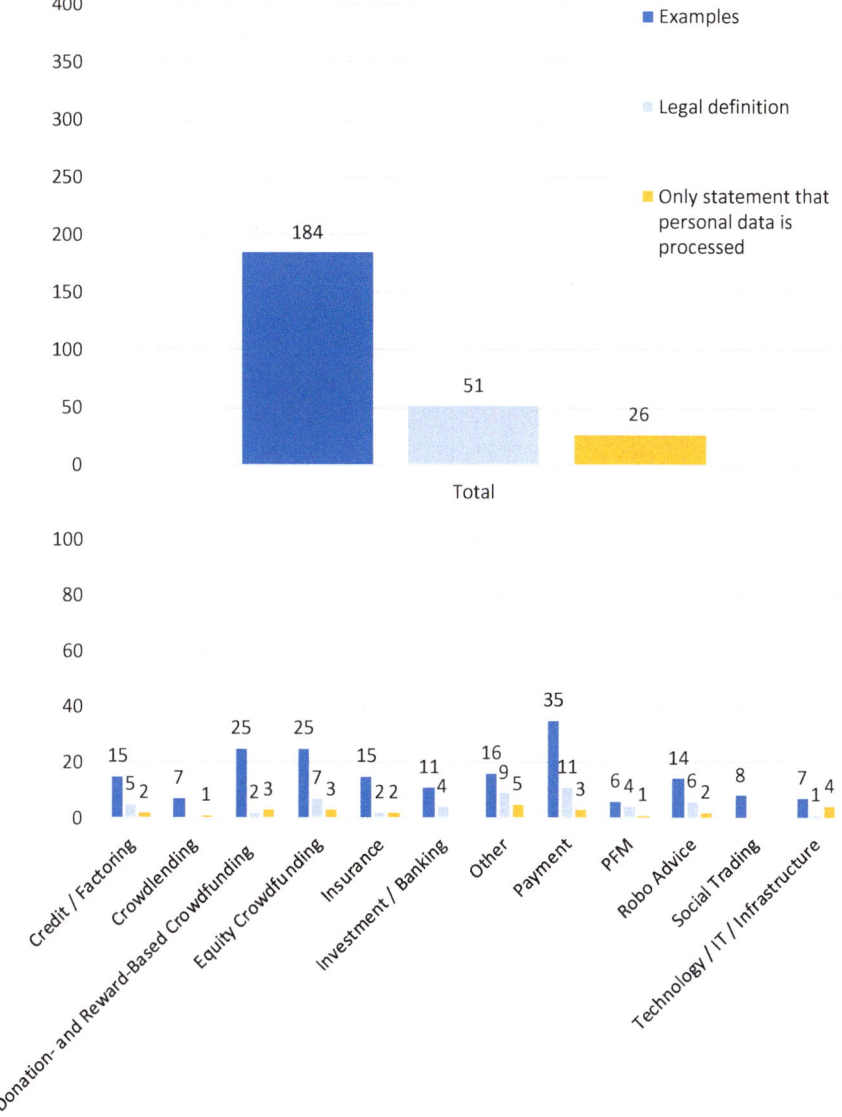

Fig. 4.5 The reasons personal data were not listed exhaustively after the implementation of the GDPR. Distinction by FinTech Segment, $N = 261$

further broken down into the individual FinTech segments in the following paragraphs.

Specifically named personal data differ for the respective FinTech segments. For a more detailed evaluation, we combined the FinTech subsegments into the following segments (see Figs. 4.8, 4.9, 4.10, 4.11, and 4.12): Payment, financing (investment and banking, donation- and reward-based crowdfunding, equity crowdfunding,

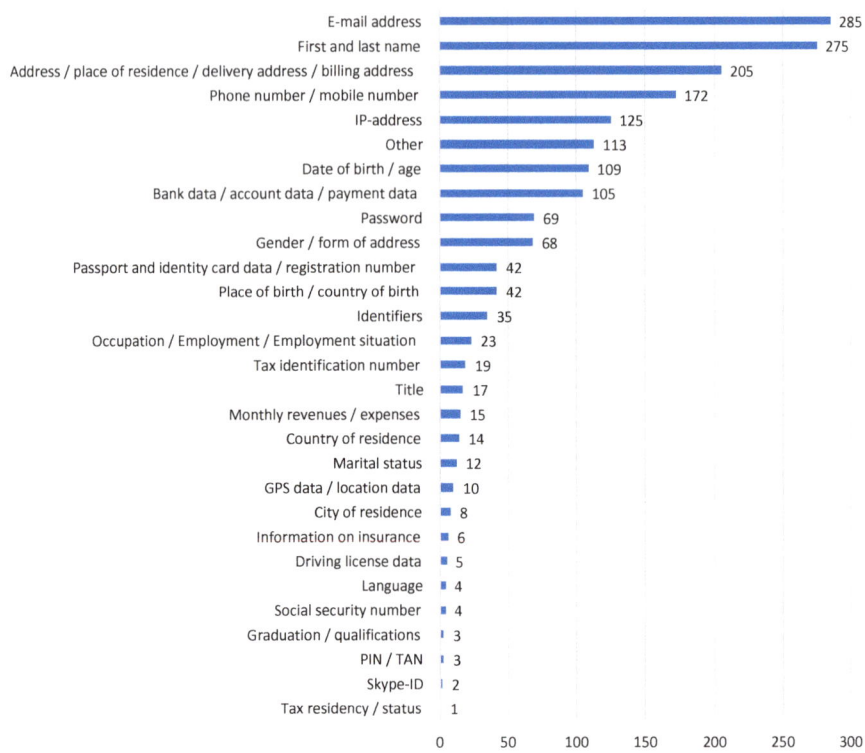

Fig. 4.6 Types of personal data processed according to the privacy statement after the implementation of the GDPR. Number of evaluated privacy statements $N = 370$

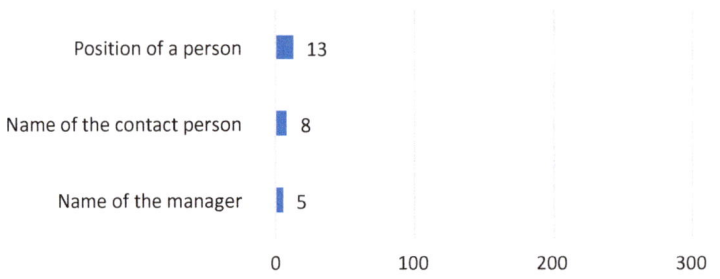

Fig. 4.7 Types of personal data related to a company that are processed according to the privacy statement after the implementation of the GDPR. Number of evaluated privacy statements $N = 370$

crowdlending, and credit and factoring), asset management (personal financial management, robo advice, and social trading), insurance, and others (technology, IT, and infrastructure and others). In the figures, the x-axis is scaled down to the population of FinTechs in this segment. In all segments, e-mail address information

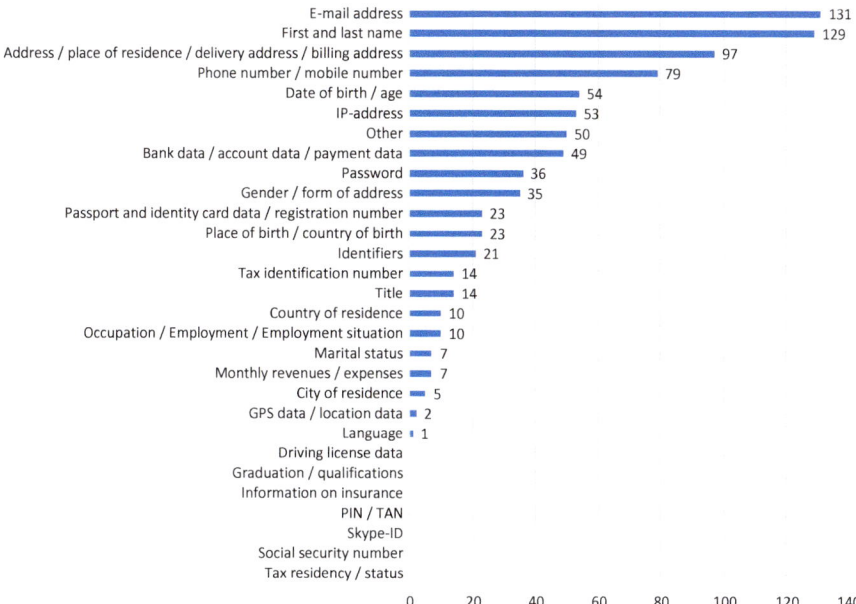

Fig. 4.8 Types of personal data processed according to the privacy statement in the financing segment after the implementation of the GDPR. Number of evaluated privacy statements $N = 220$

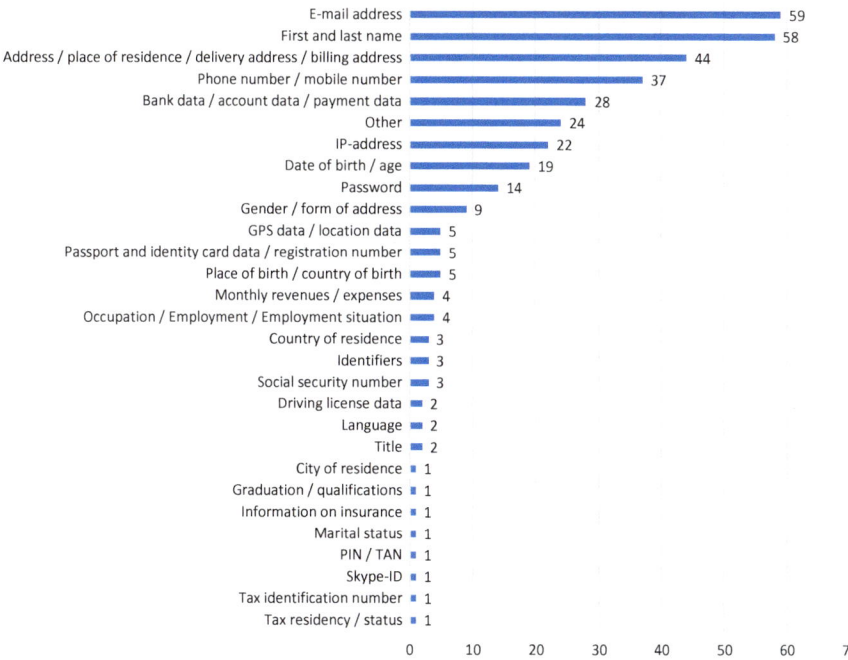

Fig. 4.9 Types of personal data processed according to the privacy statement in the payment segment after the implementation of the GDPR. Number of evaluated privacy statements $N = 104$

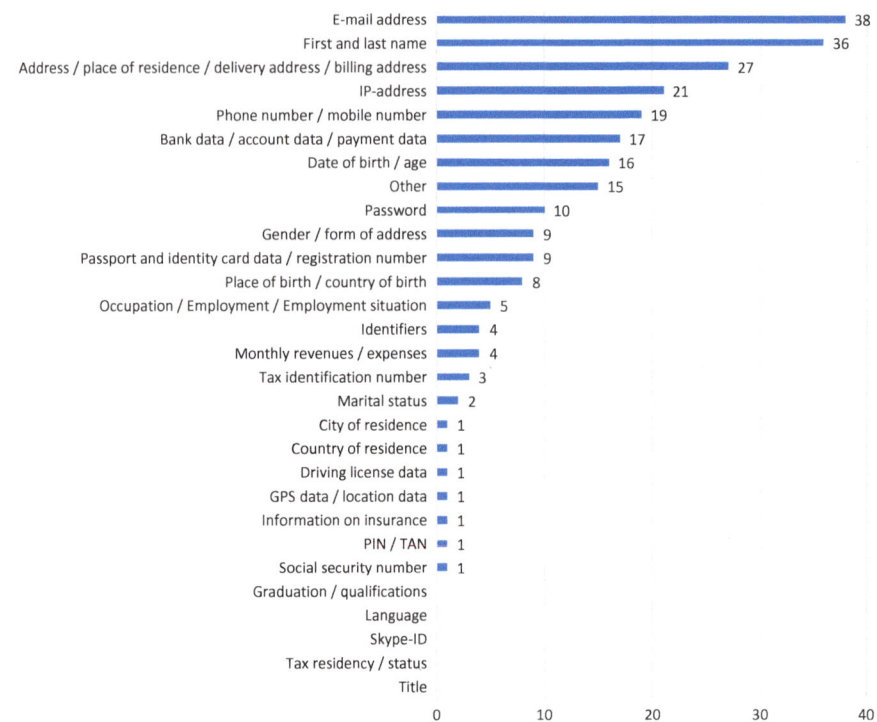

Fig. 4.10 Types of personal data processed according to the privacy statement in the asset management segment after the implementation of the GDPR. Number of evaluated privacy statements $N = 80$

is now the most frequently processed type of data instead of name. The name is now the second most frequently processed data type in each segment.

The GDPR defines special categories of personal data in Article 9 para. 1: "*Processing of personal data revealing racial or ethnic origin, political opinions, religious or philosophical beliefs, or trade union membership, and the processing of genetic data, biometric data for the purpose of uniquely identifying a natural person, data concerning health or data concerning a natural person's sex life or sexual orientation shall be prohibited.*" Some of these data continue to be processed after the reevaluation of the FinTech companies' privacy statements in 2018. In general, however, there are no significant changes in the types of personal data. All types are mentioned slightly more frequently in the privacy statements. Figures 4.13, 4.14, 4.15, 4.16, 4.17, and 4.18 give an overview of the use of particular types of personal data in the individual FinTech segments.

According to the GDPR, an enterprise is "*a natural or legal person engaged in an economic activity, irrespective of its legal form, including partnerships or associations regularly engaged in an economic activity.*" Company data do not count as personal data and therefore are subject neither to the BDSG nor to the GDPR.

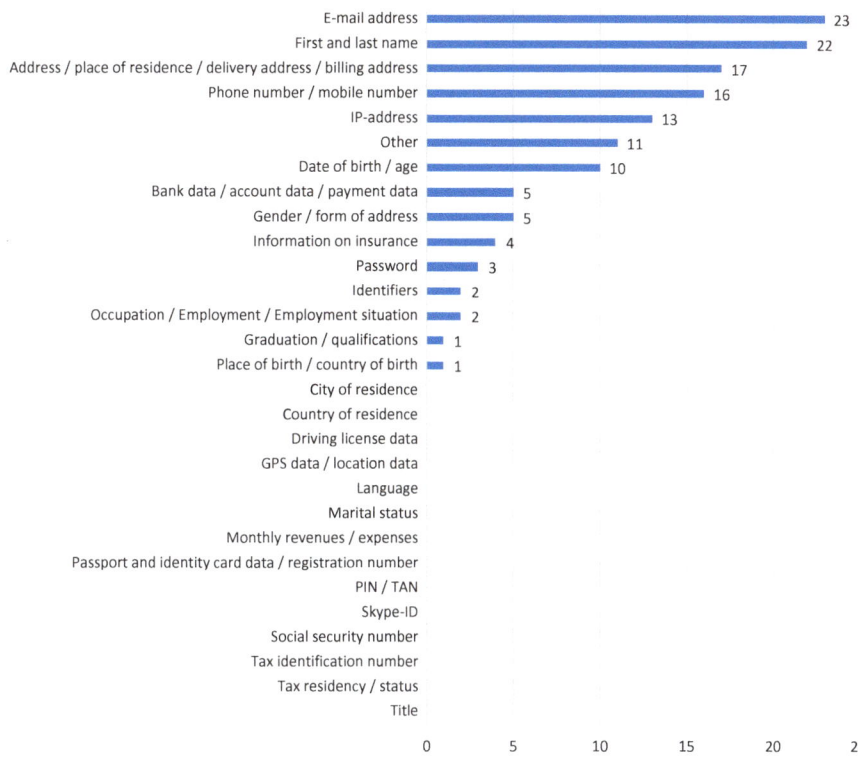

Fig. 4.11 Types of personal data processed according to the privacy statement in the insurance segment after the implementation of the GDPR. Number of evaluated privacy statements $N = 41$

However, FinTech companies process a variety of data related to a particular company. As Fig. 4.19 shows, this is still often the name of the company. The address, telephone number, and register number are now mentioned somewhat more frequently relative to the reference period of 2017.

IP addresses are also personal data. Figure 4.20 shows that 93% ($N = 343$) of the FinTech companies state that they process IP addresses of users. In the remaining cases, no specific statement is made. In the majority of cases, IP addresses are still processed to integrate web tracking services (78%, $N = 288$) and social plug-ins (26%, $N = 98$). Other reasons include newsletters, third-party content, and advertising services. Also mentioned often is the "security of the company," the need to pass on data to law enforcement authorities, or the "interests of users."

Figure 4.21 shows the purposes for which users' IP addresses are processed after the GDPR became binding according to the privacy statements. The dark blue bars indicate that the IP addresses are processed unabridged. With the exception of web tracking services, which remained more or less the same, these purposes are mentioned more often than in the reference period before the GDPR became binding. It is noticeable that no company explicitly states that IP addresses are not being

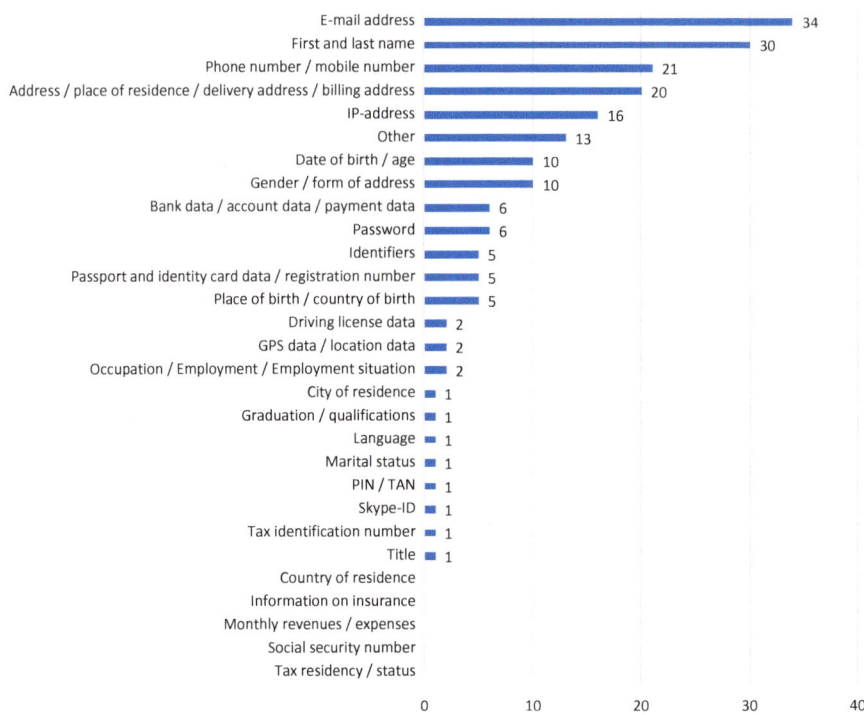

Fig. 4.12 Types of personal data processed according to the privacy statement in the other FinTechs segment after the implementation of the GDPR. Number of evaluated privacy statements $N = 60$

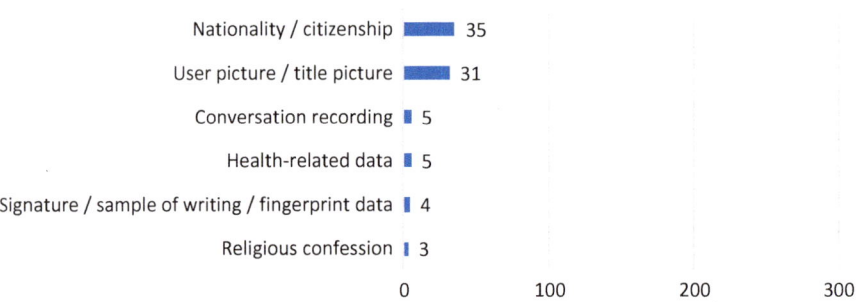

Fig. 4.13 Special categories of personal data processed according to the privacy statement after the implementation of the GDPR. Number of evaluated privacy statements $N = 370$

processed. Often no statement about IP addresses is made in the text, and only a text module for the use of Google Analytics reveals that IP addresses are being processed.

In most cases, as in the past, not only is a reason for storing IP addresses given, but reasons for processing personal data also continue to be given. Figure 4.22 shows

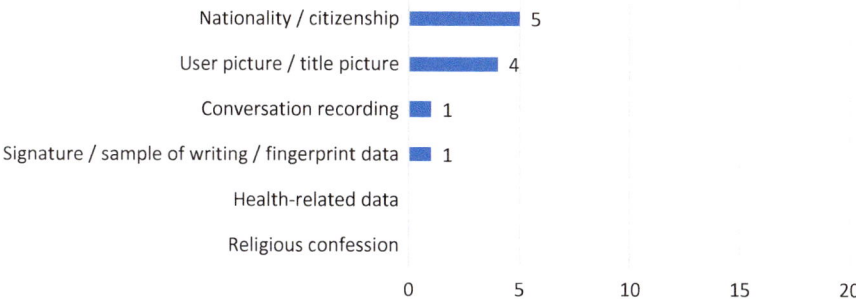

Fig. 4.14 Special categories of personal data processed according to the privacy statement in the payment segment after the implementation of the GDPR

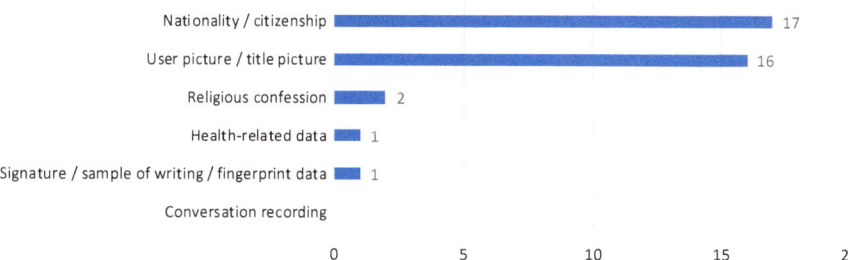

Fig. 4.15 Special categories of personal data processed according to the privacy statement in the financing segment after the implementation of the GDPR

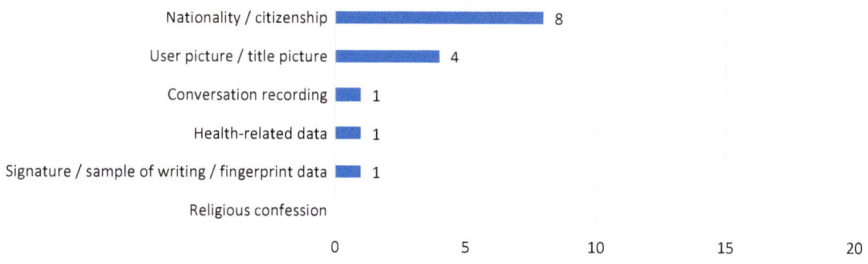

Fig. 4.16 Special categories of personal data processed according to the privacy statement in the asset management segment after the implementation of the GDPR

that 90% ($N = 338$) of FinTech companies now state a reason for processing personal data in their privacy statements. The most frequent reasons are still the need to process data for contractual purposes and to provide services to users (86%, $N = 317$). As noted in Chap. 3, this may mean making simple contact with users. The second most common reason for the processing of personal data continues to be for marketing, self- and third-party advertising, and the sending of newsletters (73%,

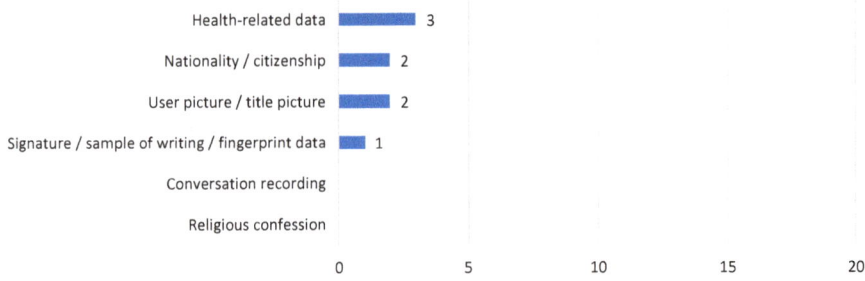

Fig. 4.17 Special categories of personal data processed according to the privacy statement in the insurance segment after the implementation of the GDPR

Fig. 4.18 Type of company-related data processed according to the privacy statement after the implementation of the GDPR. Number of evaluated privacy statements $N = 370$

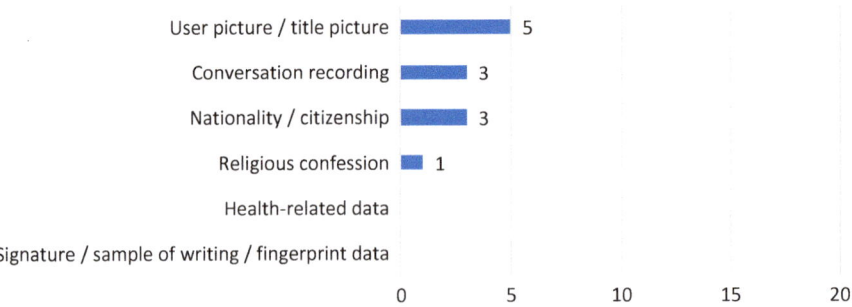

Fig. 4.19 Special categories of personal data processed according to the privacy statement in the other FinTechs segment after the implementation of the GDPR

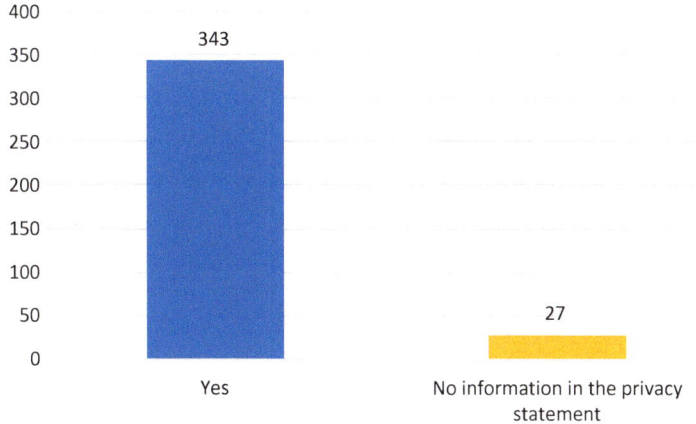

Fig. 4.20 Is the IP address processed abridged or unabridged? Or does a third party process the IP address after the implementation of the GDPR? Number of evaluated privacy statements $N = 370$

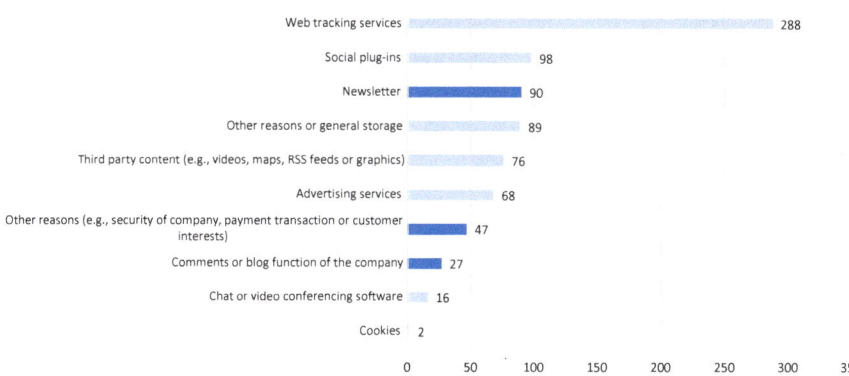

Fig. 4.21 In which context are the IP addresses of the users processed after the implementation of the GDPR? Number of evaluated privacy statements $N = 370$

$N = 232$). Customer security and compliance with legal regulations (22%, $N = 82$) and the creation of user profiles to improve the offer (16%, $N = 59$) are now of comparatively greater importance. Text modules are often used to explain why personal data are processed.[3] Figure 4.23 gives an overview of the reasons given for processing personal data.

---

[3]For example, the privacy statement of Damantis states (originally in German, translation by the authors): "Article 6 I lit. a GDPR serves our company as a legal basis for processing operations in which we obtain consent for a specific processing purpose. If the processing of personal data is necessary for the performance of a contract to which the data subject is a party, as is the case, for example, with processing operations that are necessary for the delivery of goods or the provision of

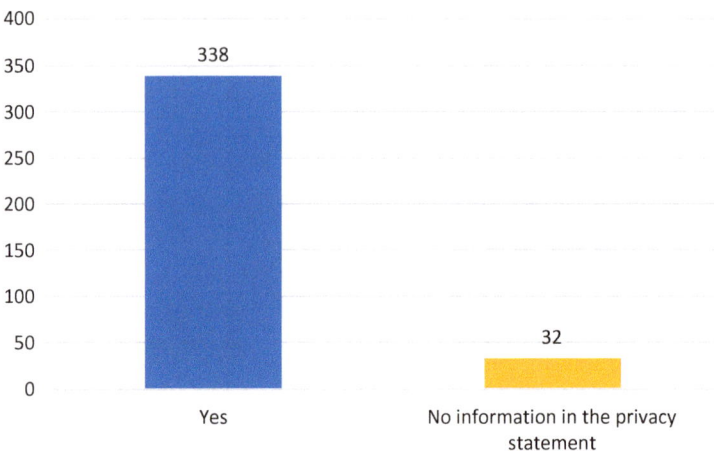

Fig. 4.22 Is a reason given for processing personal data after the implementation of the GDPR? Number of evaluated privacy statements $N = 370$

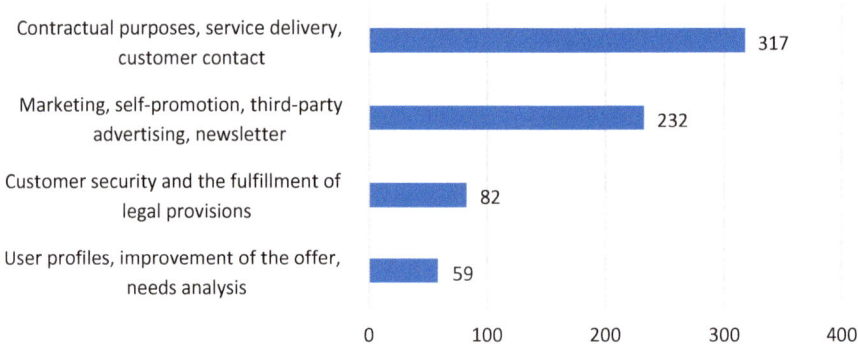

Fig. 4.23 What reason is given for processing personal data after the implementation of the GDPR? Number of evaluated privacy statements $N = 370$

---

other services or consideration, the processing is based on Article 6 I lit. b GDPR. The same applies to such processing operations that are necessary for the implementation of pre-contractual measures, such as in cases of inquiries about our products or services. If our company is subject to a legal obligation requiring the processing of personal data, such as for the fulfillment of tax obligations, the processing is based on Article 6 I lit. c GDPR. In rare cases, the processing of personal data may become necessary to protect the vital interests of the data subject or another natural person. This would be the case, for example, if a visitor were injured in our operations and his name, age, health insurance data, or other vital information would have to be passed on to a doctor, hospital, or other third party. Then the processing would be based on Article 6 I lit. d GDPR. Ultimately, processing operations could be based on Article 6 I lit. f GDPR. Processing operations that are not covered by any of the aforementioned legal bases are based on this legal basis if the processing is necessary to safeguard a legitimate interest of our company or a third party, provided that the interests, fundamental rights, and basic principles of the data subject do not predominate.

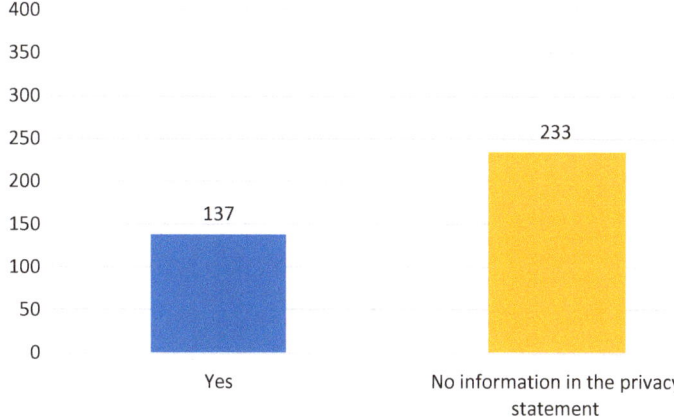

Fig. 4.24 Is it specified how long data are stored or when data are deleted after the implementation of the GDPR? Number of evaluated privacy statements $N = 370$

The GDPR defines a right of access with regard to the planned storage period of personal data or at least the criteria on the basis of which the storage period is determined. As Fig. 4.24 shows, at 37% ($N = 137$), slightly fewer FinTech companies now indicate how long users' personal data are stored. Frequently, however, reference is made to legal retention periods.[4] Very few FinTechs disclose their own deadlines and internal retention periods or data erasure cycles.

If not absolutely necessary, identification of the individual behind the processed data can be prevented under pseudonymization or anonymization. In general, the reference to pseudonymization or anonymization in privacy statements is rare and, as shown in Fig. 4.25, can now be found in 25 cases. Although this is double the number of FinTechs that undertake pseudonymization or anonymization relative to the reference period, it remains at a very low level.

In Fig. 4.26, the privacy statements are again evaluated to determine whether personal data are published. This can happen, for example, if users upload profile pictures and the online platforms publish them.

In addition, 18% ($N = 68$) of the FinTech companies that have a privacy statement now report publishing personal data, slightly more than in 2017. For the remaining 82% ($N = 302$), we find no information in the privacy statement. Personal data are published comparatively frequently in the donation- and reward-based crowdfunding (35%, $N = 16$), crowdlending (31%, $N = 4$), and personal financial

---

Such processing operations are permitted to us in particular because they have been specifically mentioned by the European legislator. In this respect, it took the view that a legitimate interest could be assumed if the person concerned was a customer of the person responsible (recital 47 sentence 2 GDPR)."

[4]For example, the privacy statement of auxmoney states (originally in German, translation by the authors): "In addition, auxmoney is subject to various storage and documentation obligations, including those arising from the German Commercial Code (HGB) and the German Tax Code (AO). The time limits for storage and documentation specified there are six to ten years."

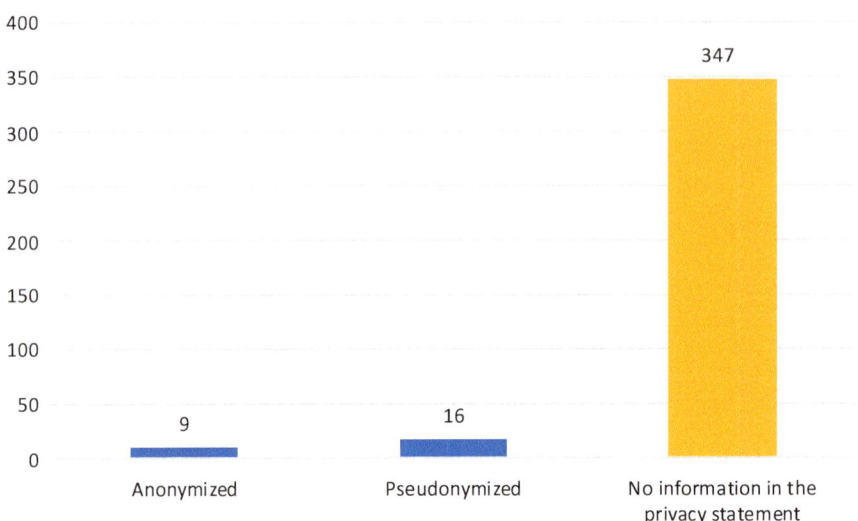

Fig. 4.25 Are data processed anonymously or pseudonymously after the implementation of the GDPR? Number of evaluated privacy statements $N = 370$

management (31%, $N = 5$) segments. Even after the GDPR became binding, the FinTech companies state that the reason for publication is that it is necessary for a commentary or blog function (57%, $N = 39$), a public or nonpublic user profile (44%, $N = 30$), or other reasons (7%, $N = 5$). In particular, the comment or blog function is now cited more frequently as a reason for publication. Figure 4.27 shows how often the reasons for the publication of personal data are mentioned.

With a share of 86% ($N = 320$), only a few more FinTech companies now state that they not only process users' personal data but also share them with third parties. As Fig. 4.28 shows, only 4% ($N = 14$) of FinTechs continue to state that they do not pass on user data to third parties. In 10% of cases ($N = 36$), it is not possible to determine from the privacy statement whether or not user data are passed on to third parties.

Even fewer privacy statements reveal what personal data of users are passed on to third parties. As Fig. 4.29 shows, only 7% ($N = 25$) of FinTech companies drew up an exhaustive list of those to whom they pass on data. A significantly larger proportion of FinTech companies (26%, $N = 98$) give at least examples of what user data are shared. Figure 4.29 also clearly shows that in most cases, even after the GDPR became binding, FinTechs do not disclose what personal data are passed on, though it is clear that they do indeed pass on data to third parties.

Figure 4.30 shows what data are shared with third parties. Frequently, this continues to include name, e-mail address, address, bank, and account, or payment data of the users. According to the information provided by the FinTech companies, this transfer is still made to ensure the fulfillment of the contract, order processing, provision of services, or out of obligations arising from the user relationship (51%, $N = 187$) and for the processing of payments or other transactions (e.g., settlement,

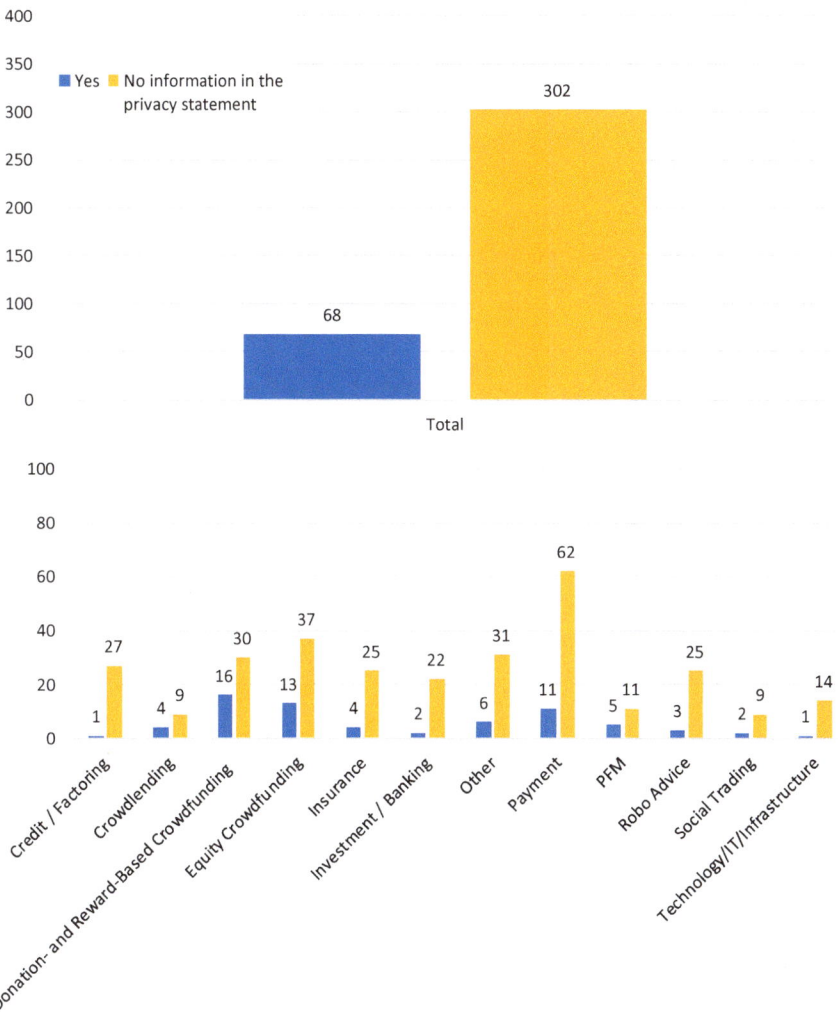

Fig. 4.26 Are personal data published after the implementation of the GDPR? Distinction by FinTech segment. Number of evaluated privacy statements $N = 370$

repayment of installments, granting of a loan, support of account transactions) (30%, $N = 111$). These reasons are mentioned slightly more frequently after the GDPR became binding. The third most common reason is no longer for advertising measures, marketing, and sending newsletters but for fraud prevention, abuse prevention, abuse identification, and risk management (15%, $N = 54$). Figure 4.31 gives an overview of the reasons for the transfer of personal data mentioned in the privacy statements.

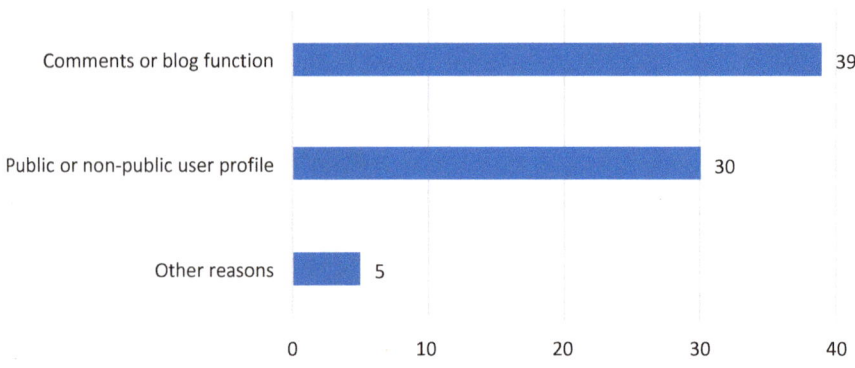

Fig. 4.27 The reasons personal data are published after the implementation of the GDPR. Number of evaluated privacy statements $N = 370$

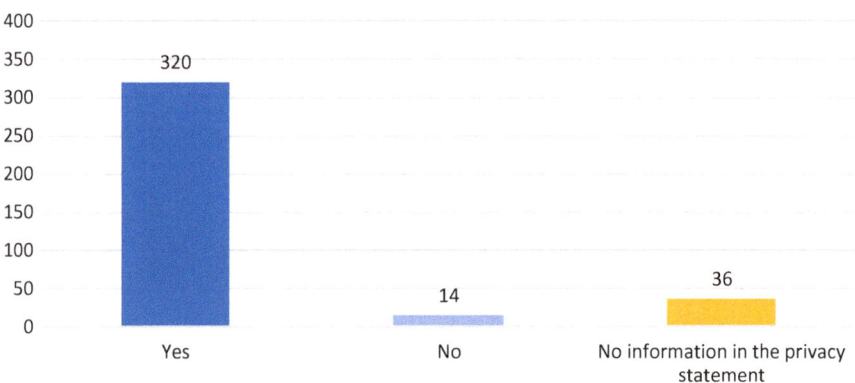

Fig. 4.28 Are personal data shared with third parties with consent after the implementation of the GDPR? Number of evaluated privacy statements $N = 370$

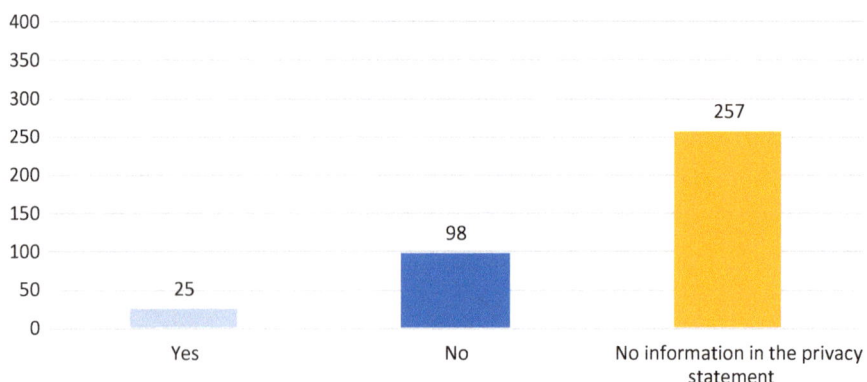

Fig. 4.29 Is there an exhaustive statement on what personal data are shared with third parties after the implementation of the GDPR? Number of evaluated privacy statements $N = 370$

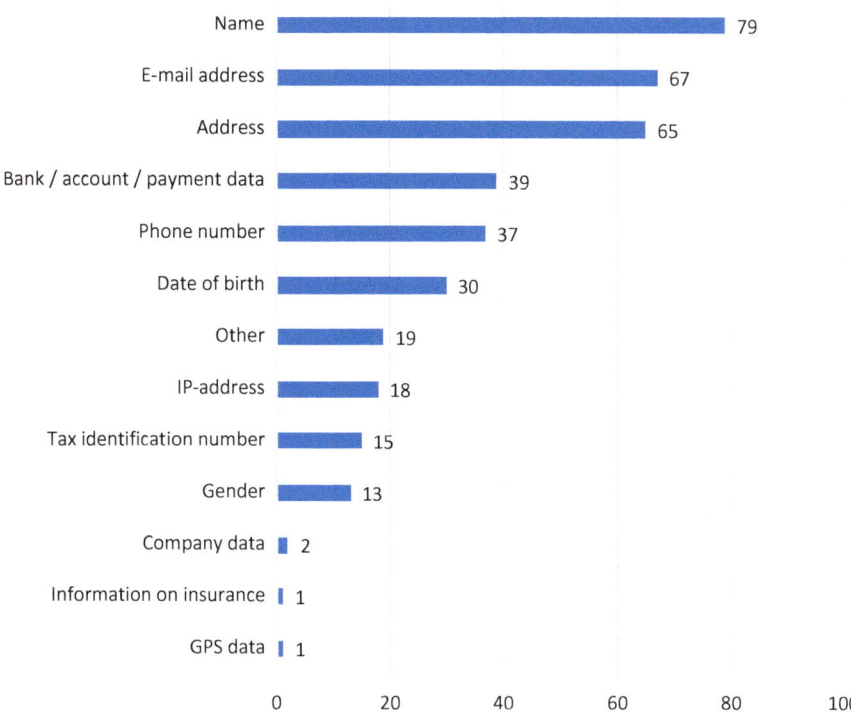

Fig. 4.30 What personal data are shared with third parties after the implementation of the GDPR? Number of evaluated privacy statements $N = 370$

When companies pass on user data to third parties, the main question is whether this is necessary for the execution of a transaction or whether this belongs to the business model of the FinTech company and is remunerated by third parties. Information on whom the data are passed to could help answer this question. Figure 4.32 shows that slightly more than half (55%, $N = 202$) of the privacy statements indicate to whom user data are shared. Compared with the time before the GDPR became binding, privacy statements have become more transparent. In some cases (12%, $N = 46$), the privacy statements now include an exhaustive list of the third parties receiving the data. Often, however, the list is not exhaustive or only business partners are mentioned (53%, $N = 196$). As Fig. 4.33 shows, 45% of FinTechs state that they pass on personal user data to third parties "only in exceptional cases." Occasionally, FinTechs also mention that data are passed on within the own company group. The proportion of FinTech companies that do not provide any information at all about which third parties receive data has risen significantly, to more than 64% compared with 2017.

In some cases, FinTechs mention not only that personal data are passed on to third parties but that personal data are also collected from third parties and linked to the data of their own users. Figure 4.34 shows that these third parties are now mentioned

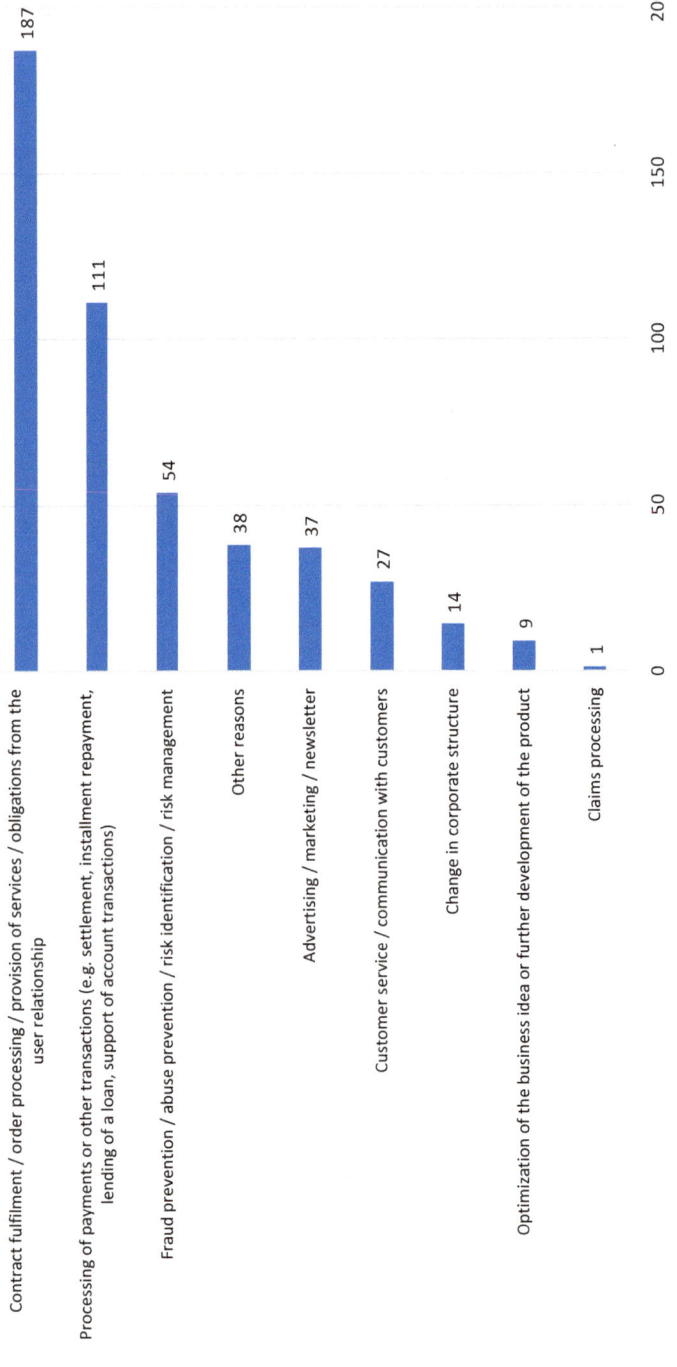

Fig. 4.31 For what purposes are personal data shared with third parties after the implementation of the GDPR? Number of evaluated privacy statements
$N = 370$

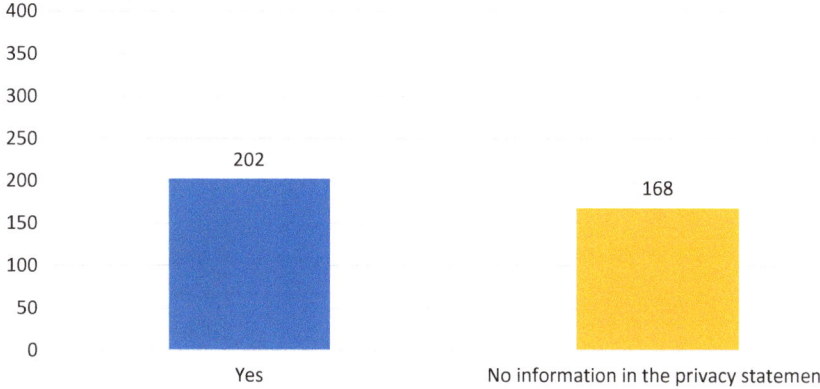

Fig. 4.32 Is it indicated to which third parties data are shared after the implementation of the GDPR? Number of evaluated privacy statements $N = 370$

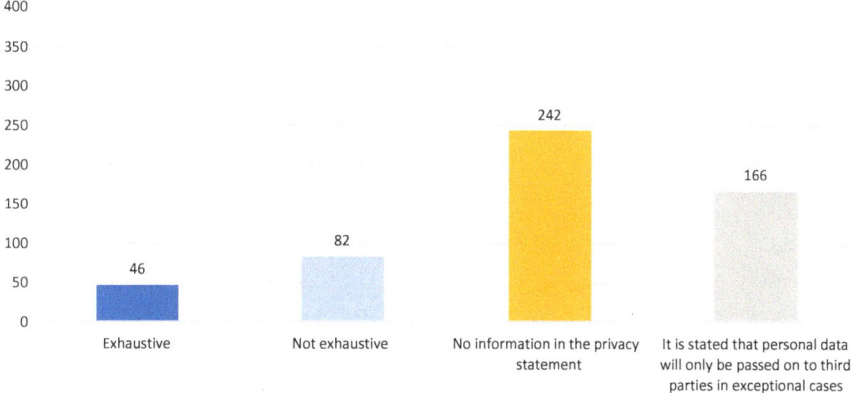

Fig. 4.33 Is there an exhaustive or nonexhaustive indication to which third parties data are shared after the implementation of the GDPR? Number of evaluated privacy statements $N = 370$

by name in even fewer cases than before (8%, $N = 31$). If names are mentioned at all, these are often Schufa Holding AG ($N = 27$), Creditreform Boniversum GmbH ($N = 17$), Bürgel Wirtschaftsinformationen GmbH & Co. KG ($N = 8$), or the Arvato Infoscore Consumer Data ($N = 5$). Some FinTechs also state that they collect additional data through social media, especially Facebook, Google, and LinkedIn.

As Fig. 4.35 shows, more than half the FinTech companies (61%, $N = 224$) now note in their privacy statements that they use social plug-ins. Social plug-ins are functions offered by third parties to disseminate the content of users or the FinTech company. Examples are the "Like" button on Facebook and the "Tweet" button on Twitter. When social plug-ins are used, information is transferred from the user's browser to the respective platform and other third parties. The FinTech companies also frequently mention that they have no influence on the transfer and no knowledge

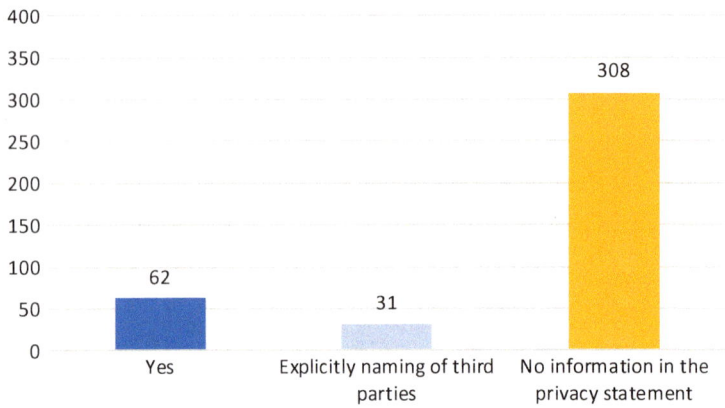

Fig. 4.34 Are personal data collected from third parties after the implementation of the GDPR? Number of evaluated privacy statements $N = 370$

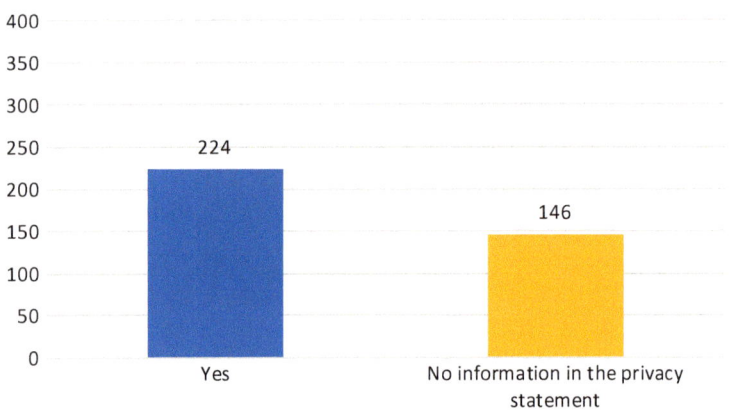

Fig. 4.35 Does the company's website use social plug-ins or are third-party services integrated after the implementation of the GDPR? Number of evaluated privacy statements $N = 370$

of the use of these data; rather, even after the GDPR became binding, the type, purpose, and scope of the data processed by third parties and their processing and use are referred to as the data protection information of the relevant third party. Figure 4.36 lists the companies whose social plug-ins are used by FinTech companies. Moreover, more than half the FinTech companies note in their privacy statement that they use a social plug-in from Facebook (52%, $N = 194$). Also especially popular are the social plug-ins from Twitter (37%, $N = 137$) and YouTube or Vimeo (29%, $N = 106$). Social plug-ins from LinkedIn, Xing, Instagram, and Pinterest are used less frequently, with less than 10% each. Google+, which was discontinued in August 2019, is still mentioned in about every fourth privacy statement.

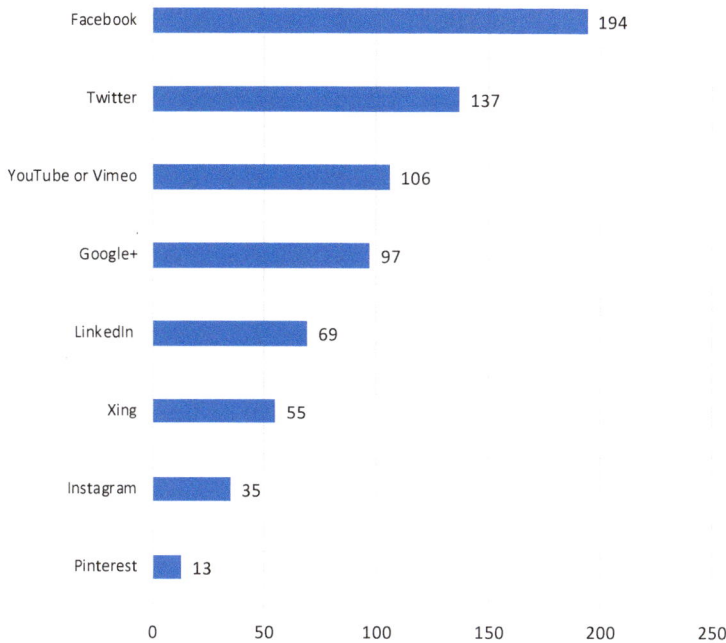

Fig. 4.36 Which third-party social plug-ins or services are used by FinTech companies after the implementation of the GDPR? Number of evaluated privacy statements $N = 370$

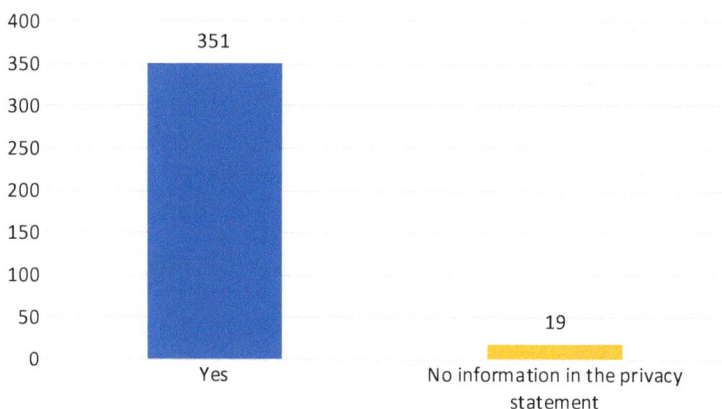

Fig. 4.37 Are behavioral, usage, or movement data processed or are tracking services used after the implementation of the GDPR? Number of evaluated privacy statements $N = 370$

As Fig. 4.37 shows, almost all FinTech companies (95%, $N = 351$) continue to note in the privacy statement that they use web tracking services to collect and evaluate data on user behavior on their websites. Web tracking enables FinTechs,

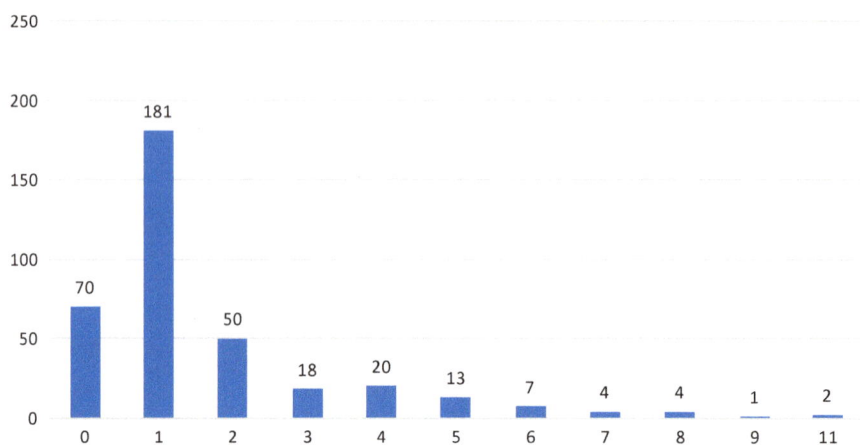

Fig. 4.38 Number of web tracking services used by FinTech companies after the implementation of the GDPR. Number of evaluated privacy statements $N = 370$

among other things, to track which websites users visit before or at the same time, what content they call up on the website, how often and for how long they view this content, and where they subsequently migrate to. Figure 4.38 shows how often one and more web tracking services are used by FinTech companies. In total, 75 different web tracking services still appear in the privacy statements. Three of four FinTech companies use Google Analytics (76%, $N = 280$). As Fig. 4.38 shows, some FinTechs continue to use up to 11 different web tracking services. Figure 4.39 lists other services mentioned by at least three FinTech companies in the privacy statement. In addition to Google Analytics, the Google Tag Manager, Piwik, Hotjar, and Zendesk are frequently used.

Advertising services such as Google AdSense or Google AdWords are still slightly less relevant than tracking services. Advertising services enable FinTechs to display advertising on web pages outside their own pages. In the analysis, the different services and additional programs from Google, Facebook, LinkedIn, and Twitter were again grouped into one category. Again, 22 advertising services could be identified in the privacy statements. Figure 4.40 shows that more than one-third of FinTech companies use advertising services provided by third parties (38%, $N = 141$). Figure 4.41 illustrates that some FinTechs continue to use up to eight different advertising services. Figure 4.42 lists other advertising services mentioned by at least three FinTech companies in the privacy statement. The services of Google, Facebook, Bing Ads, LinkedIn, Outbrain, and Twitter are frequently used. Compared with 2017, this order remained unchanged. What is striking here is that the FinTechs sometimes use different text modules for tracking and advertising services, though they use the same services.

As Fig. 4.43 shows, when adding the web tracking and advertising services together, we find that up to 15 different services are sometimes used by the FinTechs.

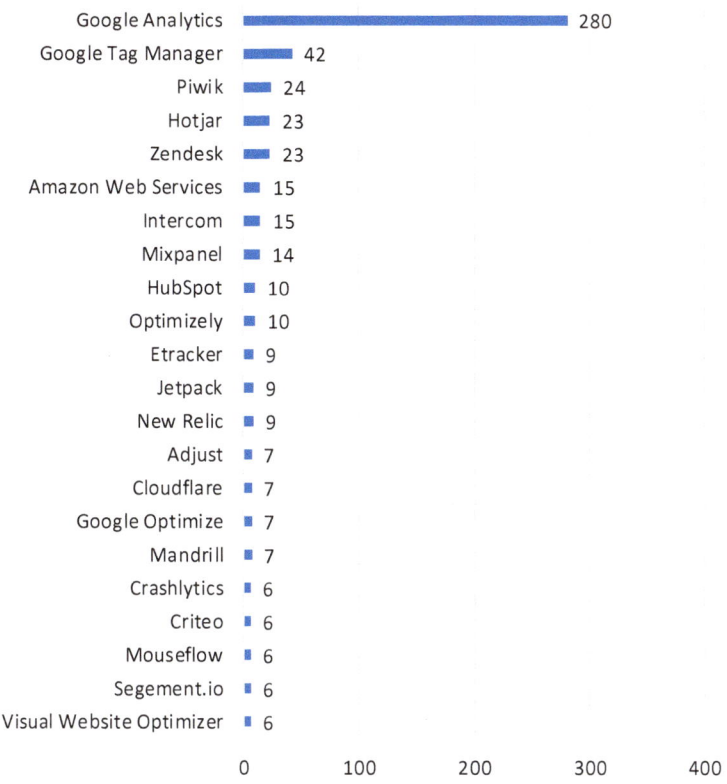

Fig. 4.39 Frequency of web tracking services used by FinTech companies after the implementation of the GDPR. Number of evaluated privacy statements $N = 370$

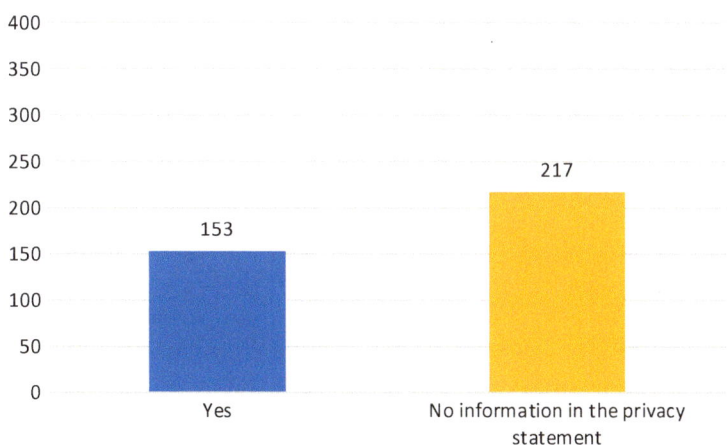

Fig. 4.40 Is third-party software used for promotional purposes after the implementation of the GDPR? Number of evaluated privacy statements $N = 370$

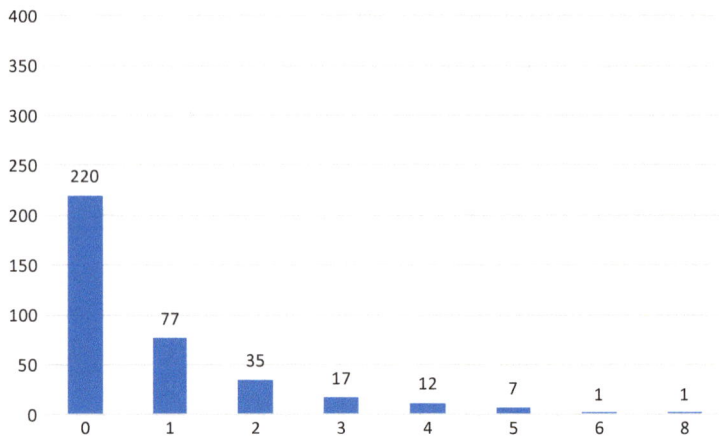

Fig. 4.41 Number of advertising services used by FinTech companies after the implementation of the GDPR. Number of evaluated privacy statements $N = 370$

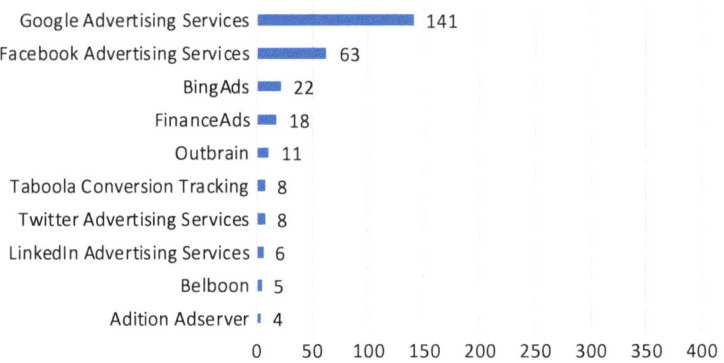

Fig. 4.42 Frequency of advertising services used by FinTech companies after the implementation of the GDPR. Number of evaluated privacy statements $N = 370$

Figure 4.44 also gives an overview of the frequency of services used in the various FinTech segments. It is clear that no FinTech segment has a particularly right-skewed distribution, and therefore the frequency with which these services are used is not segment specific.

Cookies are often used to store information associated with a website locally on a user's computer for a certain period and to transmit this information back to the server of the FinTech company on request. Cookies make it possible to individualize the use of a web page by authenticating the user when he or she returns to the respective page. In total, 86% ($N = 317$) of FinTech companies report using cookies (see Fig. 4.45). The use of cookies is therefore mentioned more frequently in the

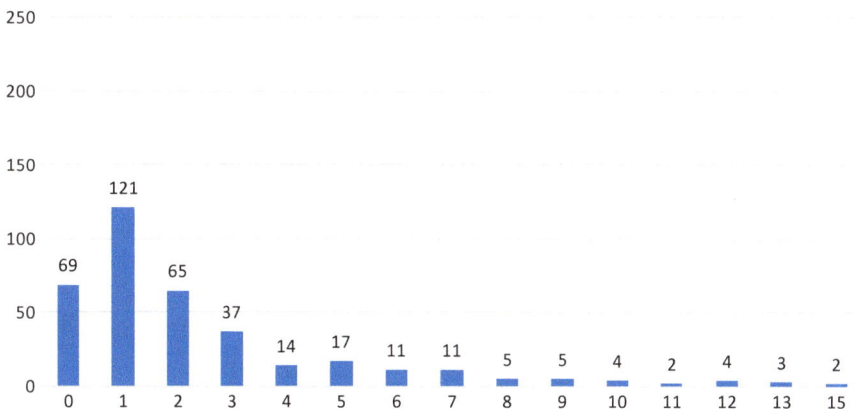

Fig. 4.43 Number of web tracking and advertising services used by FinTech companies after the implementation of the GDPR. Number of evaluated privacy statements $N = 370$

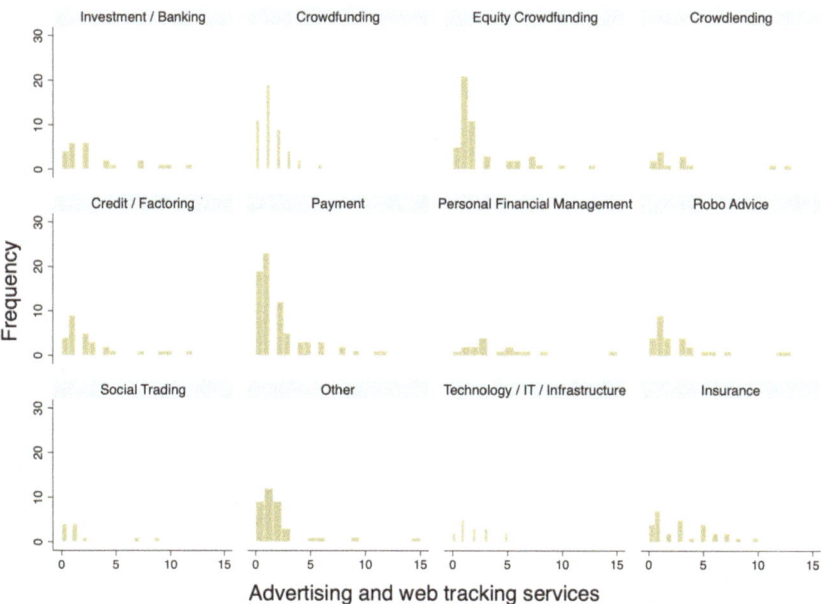

Fig. 4.44 Number of web tracking and advertising services used by FinTech companies by FinTech segment after the implementation of the GDPR. Number of evaluated privacy statements $N = 370$

privacy statements than in 2017. The remaining 14% ($N = 53$) of FinTechs do not provide any information on the use of cookies. In 46% of the cases ($N = 146$), the FinTech companies state that they store cookies permanently, which corresponds to

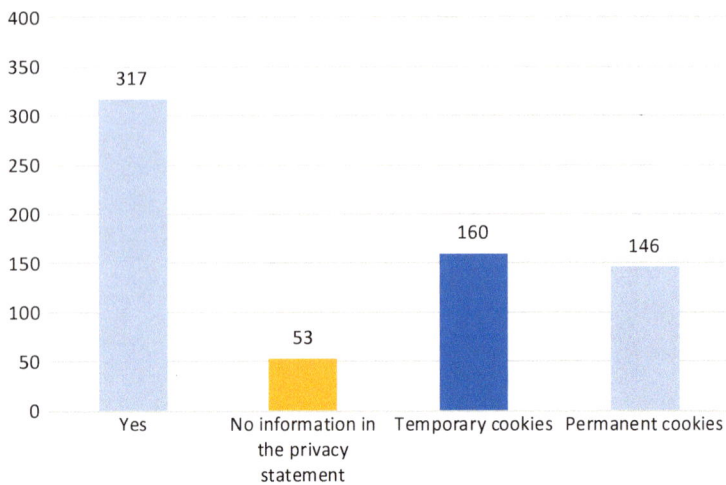

Fig. 4.45 Does the FinTech company provide information on the use of cookies after the implementation of the GDPR? Number of evaluated privacy statements $N = 370$

an increase of 15 percentage points. In 50% of the cases ($N = 160$), only temporary cookies are used, which corresponds to an increase of 13 percentage points compared with 2017. The remaining privacy statements give no information about the type of cookies used. Many companies continue to use both temporary and persistent cookies.

Data are also transmitted to the FinTech companies via server log files by means of the browser or the end device used by users. In this context, two of five FinTech companies draw up a conclusive list of the data processed (42%, $N = 157$). Another 36% ($N = 135$) at least create a nonexhaustive list, while 21% ($N = 78$) do not provide any information about the server log files. Figure 4.46 gives an overview of the data processed using log files. Figure 4.47 gives an overview of how often a list of what data are transmitted through server log files is given in the privacy statements, either conclusively or not conclusively. In the case of server log files, it is particularly noticeable that privacy statements increasingly use standardized text modules,[5] while in the period before the GDPR became binding, individualized text was still frequently added.

---

[5]For example, the privacy statement of the equity crowdfunding platform GreenVesting Solutions GmbH states (originally in German, translation by the authors): "This general data and information is stored in the log files of the server. Data processed may include (1) the browser types and versions used can be recorded, (2) the operating system used by the accessing system, (3) the website from which an accessing system accesses our website (so-called referrer), (4) the sub-sites that are accessed via an accessing system on our website, (5) the date and time of access to the website, (6) an Internet protocol address (IP address), (7) the Internet service provider of the accessing system and (8) other similar data and information used to avert dangers in the event of attacks on our information technology systems. When using this general data and information, GreenVesting Solutions GmbH does not draw any conclusions about the person concerned. This information is

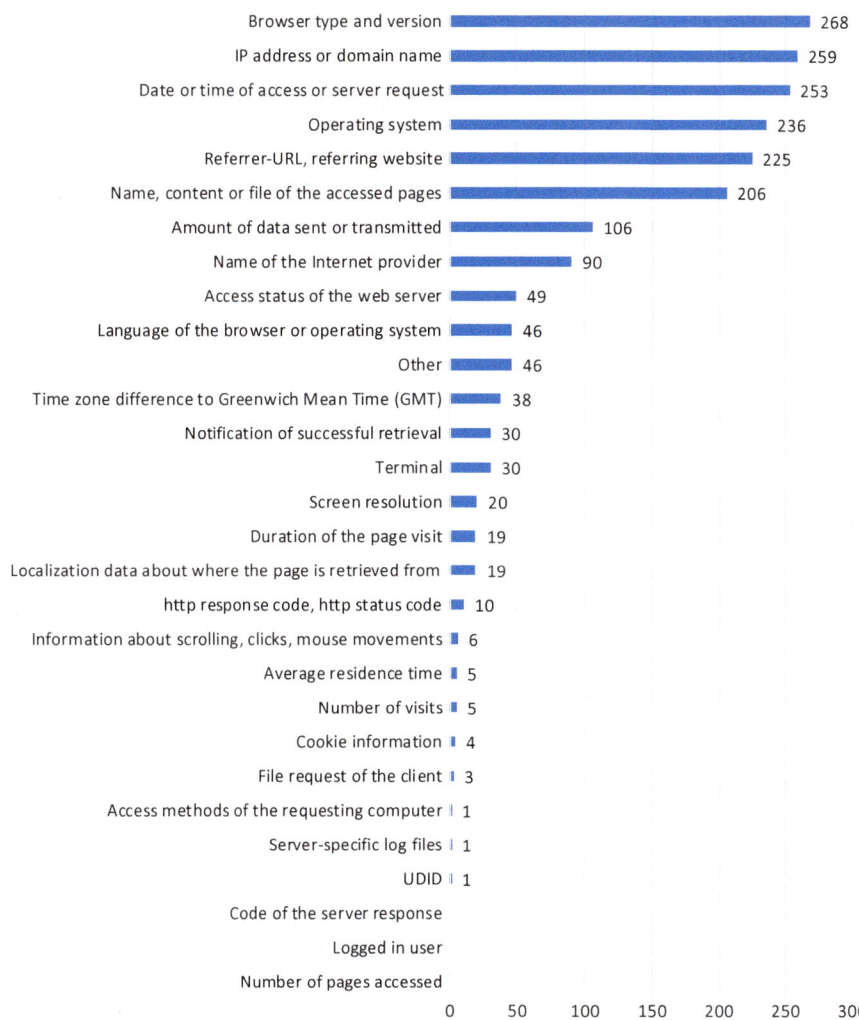

Fig. 4.46 Frequency of data processed by log files after the implementation of the GDPR. Number of evaluated privacy statements $N = 370$

needed to (1) correctly deliver the content of our website, (2) optimize the content and advertising of our website, (3) ensure the long-term functionality of our information technology systems and the technology of our website, and (4) provide law enforcement authorities with the information necessary to prosecute a cyber attack."

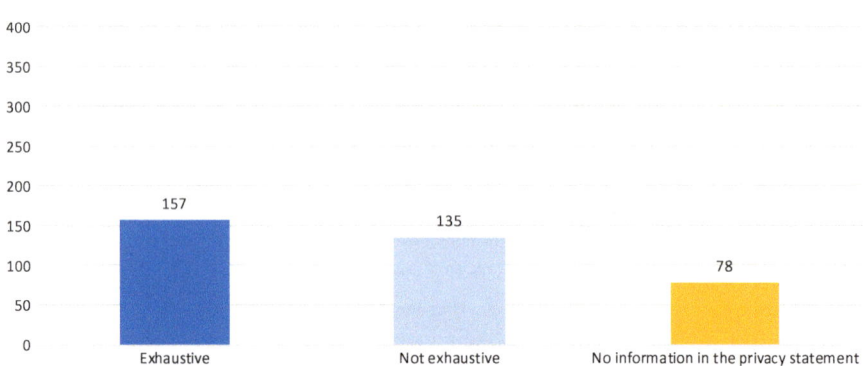

Fig. 4.47 Frequency with which the privacy statements provide an exhaustive or nonexhaustive list of what data are transmitted through server log files after the implementation of the GDPR. Number of evaluated privacy statements $N = 370$

Reference

Dorfleitner, G., Hornuf, L., Schmitt, M., & Weber, M. (2019). Marktüberblick. In F. Möslein & S. Omlor (Eds.), *FinTech-Handbuch. Digitalisierung, Recht, Finanzen* (pp. 21–38). Munich: C.H.Beck.

Chapter 5
FinTech Business Models

Abstract This chapter uses theoretical considerations and insights from expert interviews to analyze four different aspects of FinTech business models. First, we analyze the FinTechs' cooperation with banks and find that both sides can usually profit from cooperation, while in practice cooperation also can fail. In a second step, we investigate the use of big data by FinTechs. In particular, we describe some known use cases of big data in FinTechs. We find that, while the potential for big data in the financial industry is large, the use by FinTechs is not that frequent today. We also discuss legal and economic limitations of big data applications. Third, this chapter provides an analysis of the sustainability of FinTech business models. Fourth, we analyze FinTechs that specialize in the provision or brokerage of debt and loan substitutes.

This chapter deals with various aspects of FinTech business models. First, we analyze the FinTechs' cooperation with the banks. In a second step, we investigate the use of big data by FinTechs. In particular, already-known fields of application and uses of big data are described at FinTechs, and future developments of big data applications are analyzed. Third, we discuss the legal and economic limitations of big data applications. Last, we carry out an analysis of the sustainability of FinTech business models and the FinTechs that specialize in the provision or brokerage of debt and loan substitutes.

5.1 Cooperation with Banks

This chapter deals with the question of how the cooperation between banks and FinTechs should be assessed. Ever since Coase (1960) and Buchanan (1989), economic literature has stressed that voluntary cooperation under certain circumstances can lead to efficiency. One of the interviewed experts explicitly argued that the cooperation between FinTechs and banks was efficient precisely because the two market participants voluntarily agreed to work together. Of concern, however, is whether the cooperation between FinTechs and banks will also have negative external

© Springer Nature Switzerland AG 2019

G. Dorfleitner, L. Hornuf, *FinTech and Data Privacy in Germany*,
https://doi.org/10.1007/978-3-030-31335-7_5

effects at the expense of third parties. Third parties in this context could be, for example, the customers of FinTech companies or banks. A possible external effect at the expense of third parties would be if the cooperation between FinTechs and banks resulted in the exchange of customer data, thereby increasing the risk of data theft, or if a FinTech illegally resold the data, for example, to avert insolvency. However, none of these scenarios are FinTech specific but can occur in any form of cooperation with banks in which customer data are exchanged. Thus, FinTech companies must first decide whether they want to act on the market in the long run and want to increase customer benefits through innovations and technologically enhanced services.

Brandl and Hornuf (2017) examine the cooperation activities between FinTechs and banks in Germany. Using the database of Dorfleitner et al. (2017a), they analyze press releases, annual reports, and websites of banks and FinTechs and evaluate sector reports on cooperation activities from January to June 2017. Figure 5.1 gives an overview of the cooperation activities between FinTechs and banks. The results show that cooperation is primarily geared to the integration or use of a FinTech application (*product-related cooperation*). Banks often cooperate with providers of video identification processes, such as IDnow or WebID, or with providers of analysis tools, such as fino, which support credit checks or account changes by analyzing bank-related customer data. Some banks integrate social trading or equity crowdfunding applications from FinTechs into their own product portfolios. Investments in FinTechs are mainly in B2B and back-end applications. In the front-end segment, banks invest in payment service providers and FinTechs from the financing segment. Recently, robo adviser Scalable Capital received funding from the global investment management company BlackRock. In addition, banks and savings banks occasionally set up FinTech spin-offs, such as the online payment system paydirekt. Hornuf et al. (2018) show that cooperation between banks and FinTechs often occurs when banks have defined a digitization strategy or employ a chief digital officer.

According to Teece (1986, 1998), the nature of the cooperation relationship depends on how a company adopts a technology. Because the applications offered by FinTech companies are often software, integrating FinTechs into a bank does not often make sense (Brandl and Hornuf 2017). Given the high context dependency of software and the need to adapt it to the changing needs of bank customers, the product must be constantly updated. Under these circumstances, there are good reasons for banks not to buy up FinTech companies or to fully integrate them. As start-ups, FinTechs are often more flexible, faster, and more innovative than banks. If banks were to integrate FinTechs into their existing structures, FinTechs would precisely lose the characteristics that enable them to develop more customer-friendly financial products. So, banks might do well not to buy up the best FinTechs in the market.

However, the literature also notes that banks often lose their autonomy through FinTechs or TechFins because some of these companies seize banks' added value (Zetzsche et al. 2018). In this case, the added value for customers derives from the stronger competition, which leads to a reduction in prices; in addition, traditional market participants tend to open up their services to a broader circle of customers. An example of this is the robo advice offering of UBS, which has begun providing digital asset management for clients with more than GBP 15,000.

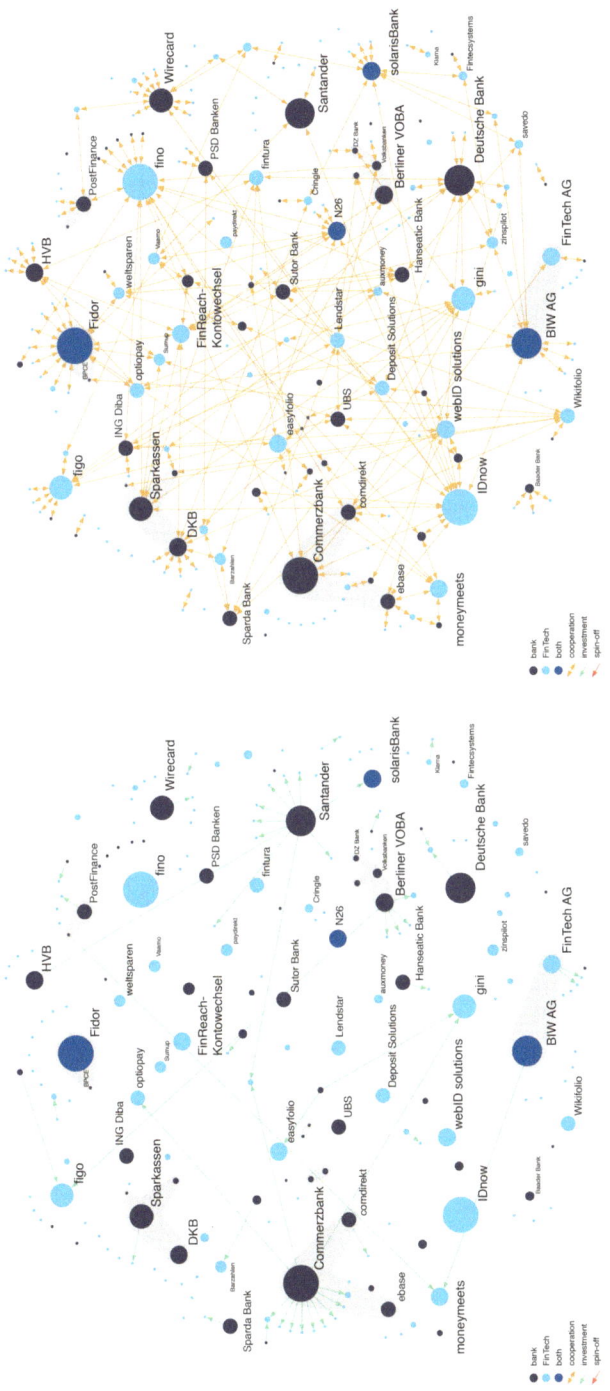

Fig. 5.1 Cooperation of FinTechs and banks in Germany (as of June 2017). With kind permission by © Brandl and Hornuf (2019), All rights reserved

After all, many FinTechs do not have a banking license and therefore must cooperate with banks. In particular, FinTechs in the financing sector that conduct commercial lending business are dependent on the license of a bank to operate their business model. An example is auxmoney, the market leader in crowdlending, whose credit business is handled by Süd-West-Kreditbank. Banks such as Fidor Bank, FinTech Group Bank, solarisBank, and Wirecard Bank have entered into cooperation with FinTech companies and frequently offer the necessary technical expertise and programming interfaces in addition to banking services. However, the possibility that FinTechs may be able to grow only to a limited extent with these banks contradicts the very reason behind the cooperation with these "API banks," as there is high demand for the corresponding services of API banks, and over time only limited resources could be made available to existing customers. For this reason, the FinTech Barzahlen has decided to cooperate with Grenke Bank. FinTechs often cooperate with traditional banks to gain advantages, as these banks are better networked internationally and are more familiar with international regulatory issues. Given FinTechs' rapid growth, the question of whether to enter into cooperation with a bank creates a conflict of objectives between technical expertise, in combination with programming interfaces and internationality, and regulatory experience.

The question of how the cooperation between FinTech companies and banks will develop in the future remains to be answered. The following three models are conceivable:

1. Banks will buy up more FinTechs. If so, the added value will not be permanent. According to Brandl and Hornuf (2017), at least in Germany, this trend has not yet been observed.
2. Both market players will divest themselves by specializing in different market segments. Even then, the added value of cooperation will not be permanent.
3. Both market players will form a lasting cooperation relationship. Here, both market participants will focus on their respective core business. In the case of such specialization, the potential added value of FinTechs will be the greatest.

The experts answered several questions on the subject of cooperation with banks. Figure 5.2 shows the answers to the question whether cooperation between banks and FinTechs creates lasting added value (question 1 in Appendix A.2).

The vast majority of respondents answered this question in the affirmative (36 responses). Only two respondents stated that the cooperation between banks and FinTechs did not create added value. In total, 31 respondents reported added value for both partners. Respondents particularly frequently noted that added value was created because FinTechs generated innovations, and thus banks would also subsequently initiate new innovations (13 responses). Nine respondents identified added value for the customer and also for the economy.

The individual respondents raised the following issues:

• Cooperation with banks would allow FinTechs to focus on generating ideas, while banks focused on implementing regulation. To some extent, FinTechs

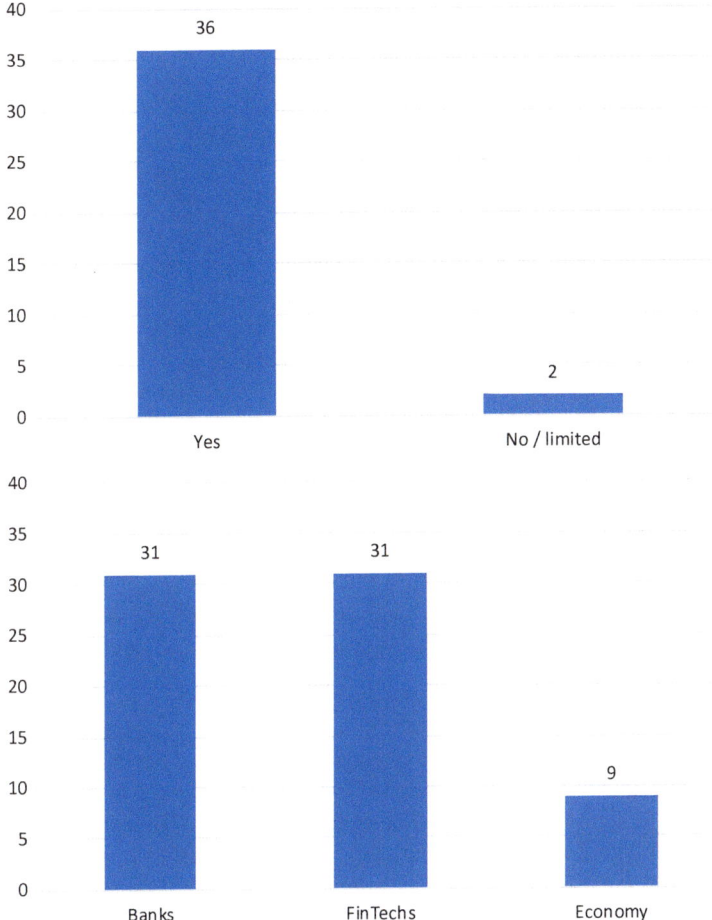

Fig. 5.2 Answers to the question of added value through cooperation between banks and FinTechs. The upper graph shows the yes/no answers, and the lower graph shows the answers on the party for which the added value would arise (multiple answers possible)

would also learn how t o implement certain regulations by cooperating with banks.

- FinTechs would benefit from access to banks' data. Another advantage is that customer confidence in the banks would transfer to FinTechs through cooperation, which would facilitate market access for FinTechs.
- For banks, the added value of cooperating with FinTechs would derive from their change of thinking and corporate culture (seven mentions). Banks would increasingly implement new projects and test new products that are more customer oriented.

- A respondent noted that FinTech bank N26 was not conceivable as a spin-off of an established major German bank and that innovations were now brought into banks from outside.
- The profitability of banks could suffer from cooperating with FinTechs. This is particularly the case if FinTechs took advantage of the profitable digital value creation from the value chain of the banks, forcing the banks to switch to relationship banking.
- The specialization and focus of banks and FinTechs would result in added value for the customer (nine mentions). Customers would also benefit from the elimination of intermediaries and the associated cost savings.
- Cooperation between banks and FinTechs might also lead to laxer security standards for customers. This would include, for example, nonexistent encryption or firewalls when using FinTech services that offer mobile payment methods.
- Cooperation between banks and service providers have had a long tradition in the financial services sector. In the past, this would have primarily affected the back office (B2B) and would have included the outsourcing of payment transactions and securities processing.
- Problems in cooperation would likely still arise from banks' problems with IT integration.
- FinTechs would likely outsource the reporting requirements to the banks. Currently, there is little standard reporting software in this area, and FinTechs could take advantage of this at banks. As a result, banks would also become B2B providers in this area.

Figure 5.3 shows the answers to the question whether banks should expand, maintain, or reduce their existing areas of business (question 2 in Appendix A.2). There was no clear agreement on this question however. The tendency to expand (six mentions) and to reduce (seven mentions) the business area was roughly evenly distributed among the respondents, whereas significantly fewer respondents

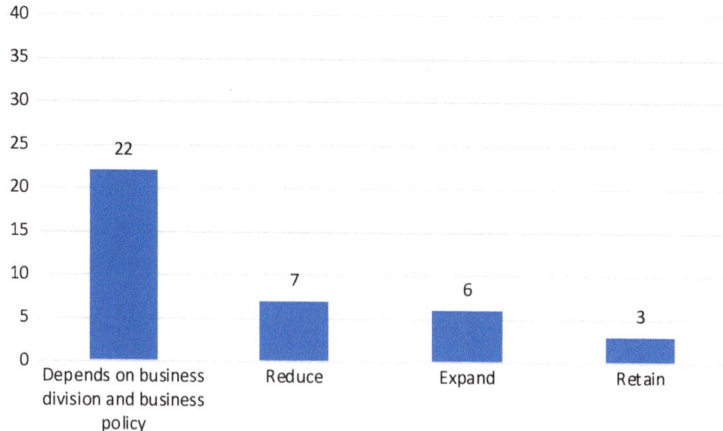

Fig. 5.3 Answers to the question whether banks should expand or reduce their business

commented that banks should retain their previous business areas or value added (three mentions). The vast majority of respondents agreed that some business would need to be expanded and others reduced, and that this decision depended on the business policy (22 mentions).

The respondents also suggested that the business areas would shift. An example is the trend from personal customer business to robo advice. A problem with expanding the business area or value creation is that banks would be threatened not only by FinTechs, which are often specialized, but also by TechFins (e.g., Alibaba, Amazon.com, Apple, Facebook, Google, Tencent), which cover a broader value creation spectrum. German banks could try to avoid this threat by also expanding their business areas or added value. Another reason for the expansion of business areas and value added is that hardly any interest is currently paid on deposits.

In concrete terms, ways to expand the business areas or add value are as follows:

- Universal banks could provide a wider range of services to their customers. For example, UBS provides small and medium-sized companies with the accounting software Bexio. This gives the bank a daily update on inventories or sales, thus enabling the granting of credit lines, possibly at better conditions.
- Specialist banks such as Deutsche Apotheker- und Ärztebank could, for example, create a vertical world of experience for their customers and offer them better products. This could involve areas such as accounting, practice management, or invoice management.
- Many banks could gain deeper insights into the delivery process of their commercial clients with the help of computers and become more familiar with their clients' processes. This would enable them to take on the insurance of risks and other business areas or added value.
- Expansion would also allow for many new opportunities to assist private customers. For example, Hamburger Sparkasse offers concert tickets for purchase. However, such offers are still the exception to date.
- Banks could also offer product bundles, such as linking a customer account to electricity or telephone providers. An example of this is O2's offer that gave customers additional data volume or an Amazon voucher for card transactions. The FinTech Barzahlen already cooperates with utility companies such as E.ON and Stadtwerke Düsseldorf.
- A caveat is that antitrust and financial market law will likely set natural limits to the expansion of business areas.

According to the respondents, the trend toward API banking is the main reason for the reduction in the number of business areas. Accordingly, banks should specialize in optimizing interfaces and reduce direct contact with customers. In line with the quote attributed to Bill Gates that "banking is necessary, banks are not," some respondents predicted that banking services would only be a commodity produced for FinTechs and other professional players in the future. Another argument in favor of reducing the number of business areas or value added was that a broad range of services is associated with high regulatory costs.

As this discussion suggests, there will likely be a greater variety of providers of financial services in the future. Banks will develop and offer independent new solutions, while FinTechs will compete with banks in certain business areas and cooperate with banks in others. Both can be beneficial for customers. In addition, new market participants, in particular TechFins, will enter the market with data-driven financial services. Although which type of provider will win the race for customers is by no means clear, what is certain is that financial services are network goods, and therefore market consolidation is inevitable.

Figure 5.4 shows the experts' answers to the question about which areas FinTechs should outsource the value creation and which areas they should create value

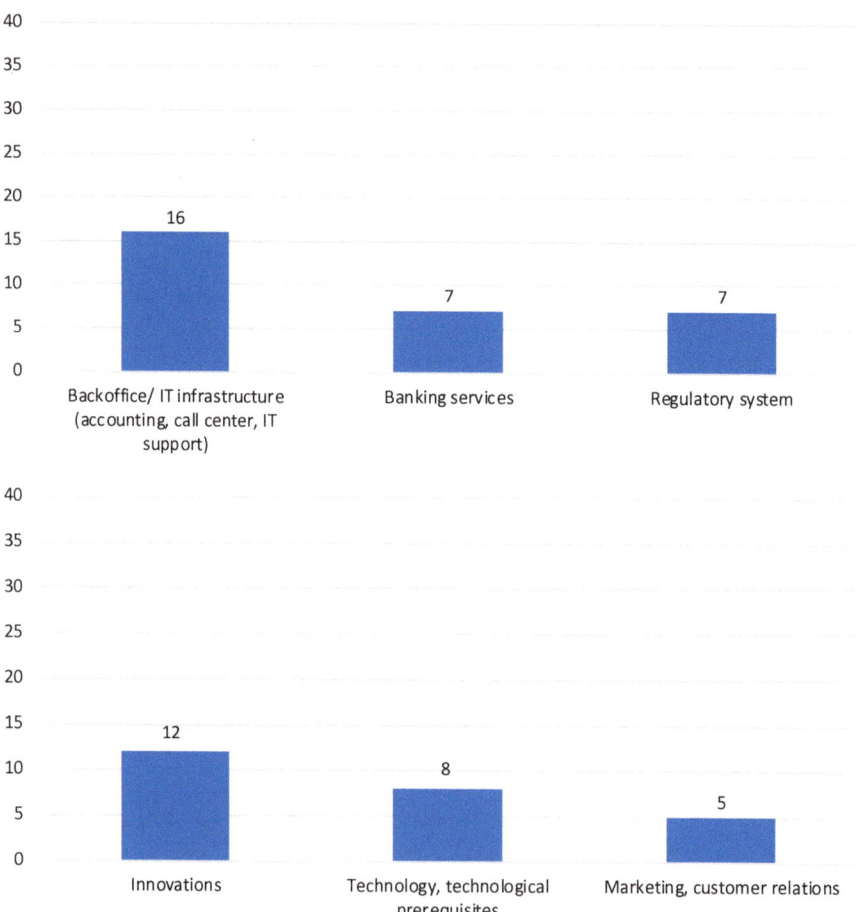

Fig. 5.4 Answers to the question of outsourcing at FinTechs. The upper graph shows the mentions of the areas that are eligible for outsourcing, the lower graph those in which the FinTechs should create value themselves

themselves (question 3 in Appendix A.2). Among the areas to be outsourced, the respondents frequently mentioned the back office and IT infrastructure (16 mentions). Seven respondents indicated that FinTechs should outsource value-added areas subject to strong regulation, such as the assumption of credit risk or other banking services. The interviewees cited the creation of innovation (12 mentions) as a self-implementing added value (though this area remains somewhat abstract), the implementation of technology or technological prerequisites (eight mentions), and marketing and customer relations (five mentions).

The respondents also suggested the following:

- Banking services (e.g., lending) that require a specific license should not be provided by FinTechs themselves but should be outsourced (seven mentions).
- The intensity and costs of regulation and licensing requirements (e.g., from the German Banking Act and Payment Services Supervision Act) were decisive for whether a service should be outsourced or not (seven mentions).
- In general terms, a company should generate the added value itself if a market transaction would be associated with comparatively higher costs. Conversely, value-added activities that can only be provided by the company at comparatively high costs should be outsourced.
- The outsourcing decision in FinTechs is a dynamic process.
- A FinTech's decision about whether to apply for a banking license might change over time. For example, the equity crowdfunding company Bergfürst initially owned a banking license but later returned it, while the FinTech N26 initially relied on Wirecard Bank's banking license but now owns one itself.
- In general, FinTechs should outsource the hosting of the infrastructure, while banks should almost never outsource it.
- The outsourcing of software and infrastructure services through SaaS or IaaS is already standard procedure at FinTechs. An example is Amazon Web Services.
- Communication, authentication, and other specialized services should be outsourced by FinTechs.
- In the case of aggregator models, in which FinTechs combine certain services into a modular overall product, outsourcing of actual banking services is an essential part of the business model.

With regard to the questions about which value creation FinTechs should outsource and which they should generate themselves, the costs and competitive advantages traditionally represent decision criteria on whether a company should outsource certain value-added areas or not. However, the social acceptance of these decisions can sometimes stand in the way of economic efficiency. For example, the use of Amazon Web Services and the associated storage of customer data outside Europe may be perceived as a competitive disadvantage in the eyes of users, despite cost savings.

5.2 Fields of Application and Uses of Big Data at FinTechs

Big data are data that are too large or too complex to be evaluated using conventional methods of data analysis (Bachmann et al. 2014). The term "big data" is often used synonymously with big data analytics, i.e., the analytical evaluation of large amounts of data.

In addition, companies whose business models are strongly linked to the Internet now tend to define the term less narrowly and generally refer to big data as the technology for collecting and evaluating digitally generated data (Baron 2013). These companies clearly also include FinTechs. The targeted evaluation of data can serve the purpose of descriptive analytics, predictive analytics, or even prescriptive analytics (Chamoni and Gluchowski 2017). We also follow the less strict concept of the term, which no longer necessarily refers to the extreme volume of the data, in this book.

In principle, companies can use big data analytics to link users' data with other data sources and then, depending on the specific situation, offer them a product they need most (Schwarz 2015). We refer to this process as customer targeting. In particular, large digital ecosystems such as Amazon.com or Google, which sell or at least broker all kinds of goods and services, can cover a broad spectrum of needs. Although FinTechs can theoretically do the same, most are still limited in offering data-based services. An example is a marketplace lending platform that uses big data analytics to determine whether a customer actually needs a more suitable current account. However, the FinTech cannot offer a current account to her or him because it is not yet part of the product portfolio. For this reason, the more services a service provider can offer, the more successfully customer targeting can be. This is most likely the case in API banking or for classic universal banks. Platforms that are dedicated to corporate financing and offer or at least broker several different financial services can also create certain customer benefits and therefore integrate this type of big data application into their business model.

Eck (2017) mentions the following further applications of big data in the FinTech sector:

- Big data based on payment transaction data provide insight into future customer behavior and can be used for customer targeting of merchants. For this purpose, customer data must be passed on by FinTechs, though customers must consent to this (see Chaps. 3 and 4).
- Big data based on payment transaction data can also help banks retain customers by recognizing when a customer is about to switch to another provider.
- Big data make it easier to identify criminal activities. Both fraud detection and the use in anti-money-laundering measures should be considered here, though the latter is particularly important for compliance departments in banks.

Big data are also used in credit scoring and credit risk management (Yan et al. 2015). Personalized product development that goes beyond pure targeting, in which products and services are developed to meet the actual or anticipated needs of customers, is another application in the FinTech area (Dapp 2015).

According to Gimpel et al. (2016), only 22% of 120 investigated German FinTechs use data analytics despite its diverse fields of application. This is a clear indication that big data do not yet play a major role in the FinTech sector today. A reason for this could be that in developed countries such as Germany, credit scoring can easily be carried using bank account transactions, and since the Second Payment Services Directive, customers can now make their data easily accessible via API interfaces by giving their consent. Data on social media such as Facebook and Twitter seldom add value to the credit scoring of German bank customers. However, the situation is different in emerging economies, in which there is no or only insufficient register or bank data. In these countries, credit scoring based on big data applications can offer real added value by providing people with sometimes cheaper financing they would not have received without these applications. However, this market does not exist in Germany, as financial data have higher explanatory power.

The results of Brandl and Hornuf's (2017) empirical study show that the component "Tech" (i.e., the technology) is not in the foreground of the overall German FinTech market. Rather, the most important factor is the improvement of business processes and applications for end customers. This is in line with the findings of Lerner et al. (2015), who show that patents related to financial innovation are often of lower quality when criteria such as the citation of scientific papers are used. A reason could be that fewer innovations are related to financial services published in scientific journals. The likelihood that German FinTech founders rely primarily on the business model and not technological developments is also reflected in their earlier employment history. More than one-quarter of FinTech founders had previously worked in the banking or insurance sector. One-fifth worked in consulting firms and may have already been involved in projects related to financial markets. Only 15% of the founders had previously worked in the IT sector, and 6% founded their companies directly after attending university. Brandl and Hornuf (2017) argue that the development of software is generally context dependent and therefore knowledge of the existing infrastructure and processes of a bank or insurance company is essential for many FinTech founders. Because APIs are often not standardized, knowledge about how they work can be helpful.

Brandl and Hornuf (2017) also show that 92% of the FinTech founders in Germany have a degree from a university or college and 14% even have a doctoral degree. This suggests that many FinTech founders do not start out from necessity (*necessity entrepreneurship*) but see an opportunity to make a profit (*opportunity entrepreneurship*). For example, Tamaz Georgadze, the founder of the FinTech Weltsparen, graduated from high school at the age of 12 and completed his studies at the age of 15. He began his doctoral program a year later at the University of Giessen. However, most of the founders (55%) have a degree in business or economics, not in one of the MINT (mathematics, information technology, natural sciences, and technology) subjects. The founders in different FinTech segments, however, had different study focuses. For example, founders in the equity crowdfunding segment had above-average media affinity, while in the robo advice segment, founders with a degree in science or IT were more frequently active.

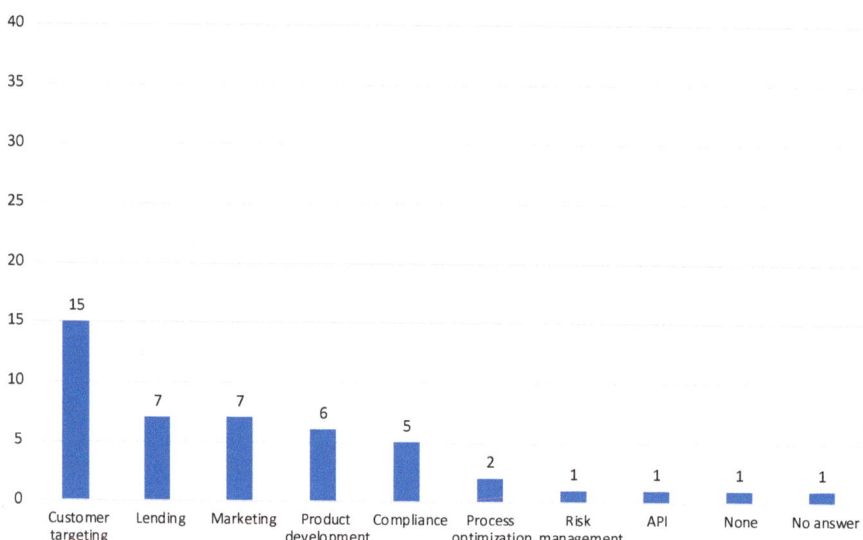

Fig. 5.5 Answers to the question of how big data can be used at FinTechs (Multiple choices possible)

In the interviews for this book, the experts were asked about the possible uses of big data at FinTechs (question 10 in Appendix A.2). Figure 5.5 shows the answers. Although some of the respondents used different terms, we subsume these for evaluation under the following umbrella terms:

- *Customer targeting*: This term refers to the most common application of big data in the Internet economy (i.e., the more targeted provision of services that customers need).
- *Product development*: The aim of this big data application is to offer personalized services to customers or to specifically develop new products to meet their needs.
- *Marketing*: This term is used in connection with better general knowledge of the market and opportunities of own products in the market.
- *Lending*: This term includes customer rating and credit scoring, credit decisions, and credit risk pricing. There are also applications here for debt collection companies.
- *Compliance*: This term includes the areas of fraud detection, compliance with anti-money-laundering regulations, and customer verification.
- Other individual answers to this question include process optimization, API banking, and risk management.

Most respondents answered the question whether there are legal and economic restrictions for big data at FinTechs (question 11 in Appendix A.2, see also Fig. 5.6) in the affirmative by mentioning legal restrictions (31 mentions). With regard to the economic restrictions, nine respondents did not give an answer, but the remainder were distributed more or less evenly between rejection and approval.

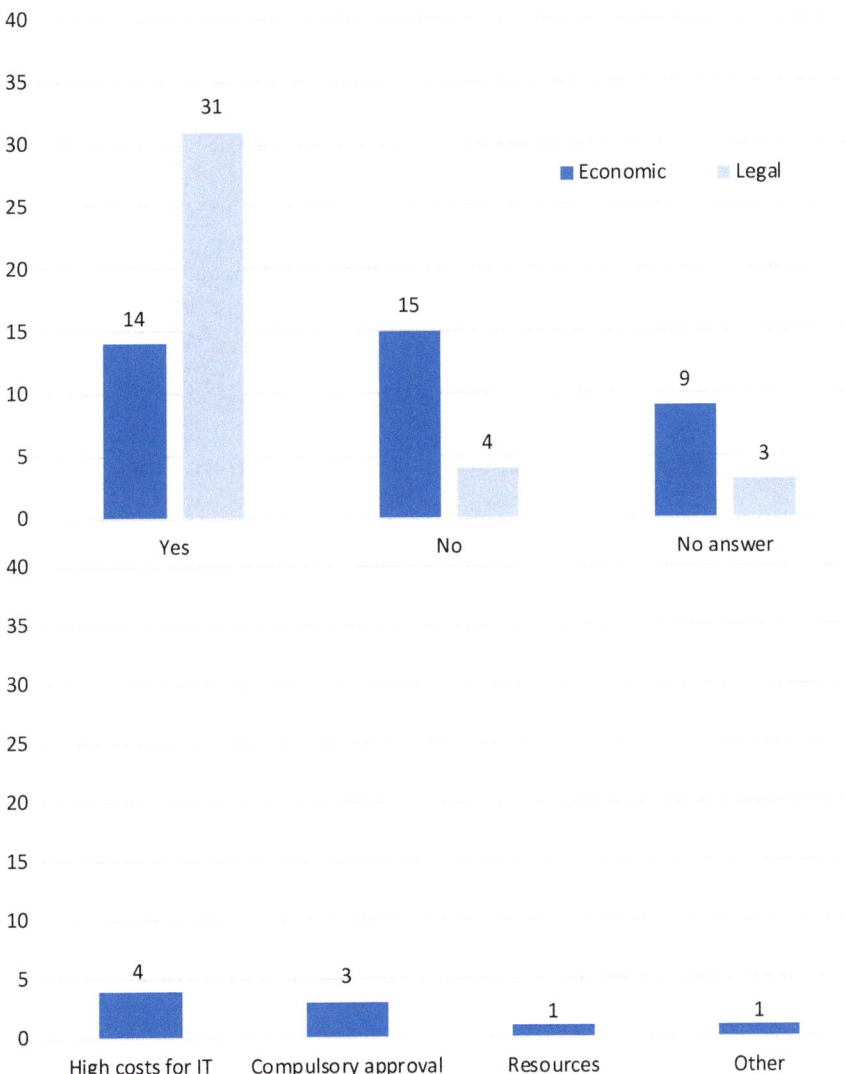

Fig. 5.6 Answers to the question of big data limitations at FinTechs. The upper chart shows answers to the question whether there are legal and economic restrictions for big data in FinTechs, the lower chart includes concrete economic restrictions mentioned

Respondents who perceived legal restrictions often mentioned data protection regulations (24 mentions) and frequently referred to the GDPR. Other references included unclear regulation, the Consumer Credit Directive, content restrictions on terms and conditions, competition law, copyright law, and patent law. With regard to the economic limitations, four respondents mentioned that the IT costs and programming costs associated with big data applications might be too high and that customers might need to agree to big data applications but actually have no power to refuse.

In summary, regarding the subject of big data at FinTechs, numerous applications already exist, some of which are of central importance for FinTechs. For other FinTechs, it is simply a matter of reaching customers more effectively and efficiently. In either case, there are restrictions on the use of big data at FinTechs, but these essentially consist of compliance with data protection laws. This may seem to be an obstacle for companies, but it is essential for customers. This is all the more true given that some customers of FinTech services do not believe they have any choice in the use of their data and so agree to it anyway, even though they do not actually support the use. Data protection regulations can provide at least minimum protection here. Economic limitations are that corresponding data or resourceful programmers cannot be found, and therefore value-generating evaluations are associated with excessive costs.

In conclusion, few FinTechs in Germany use big data analytics at all. Among those that have implemented big data applications, most only use them to improve processes such as customer communication. Only a few FinTechs have an original big data-based business model, such as Kreditech, which uses big data-based algorithms to assess the creditworthiness of individuals and to grant loans. For data protection reasons, however, these activities do not happen in Germany. According to the experts, training on the algorithms Kreditech uses occurred abroad. A possible reason could be that in Germany, basic information such as the regular payment of rent are more meaningful than big data algorithms for credit scoring. In this respect, the importance of big data is assumed but should not be overestimated for the sector as a whole. That may change in the future. After all, many FinTechs collect data from their users, even if they do not really utilize the data right now. Finally, how much more potential big data will have for FinTechs depends on the further implementation of regulations. However, the data protection needs of customers will undoubtedly continue to constitute a legitimate limitation.

5.3   Analysis of the Sustainability of FinTech Business Models

To analyze the sustainability of FinTech business models, we systematize the business models. First, a distinction can be made between B2B (business-to-business) and B2C (business-to-consumer) models. Frien (2017) defines B2B FinTechs as those that work with corporate customer business. This definition is not useful for the purpose of this book, however, because a B2B FinTech defined in this way can also provide services directly for end customers and must offer the cooperation partner a customer benefit. For our consideration, B2B FinTechs are therefore only those that fall under technology, IT, and infrastructure in the classification of Fig. 2.1, such as a provider of back-end blockchain solutions or white-label software for crowdfunding providers. Thus, these FinTechs are primarily about generating value for banks and other FinTechs. As this only concerns a minority of the German

FinTechs and the business models are more similar to those of other technology and software companies, we exclude them in the following analysis.

Second, for the business models of FinTechs that deal directly with end customers, whether private individuals or corporate customers, we follow the analysis of Gimpel et al. (2016), according to which the dimensions *interaction*, *data*, and *monetization* are relevant. Interaction distinguishes between the type of interaction (intermediary, marketplace, or bilateral) and whether it is personalized or nonpersonalized. In the data dimension, the categories *origin*, *use*, and *time horizon* exist. With regard to monetization, Gimpel et al. (2016) distinguish among the categories of end customers (paid with data, through attention, or with money), business partners (paid with money or not at all), and payment rhythm (transactional, regular, or no payment).

By applying these dimensions to real FinTechs, Gimpel et al. (2016) derive the following eight business model types for FinTechs:

Type 1: No money service. These FinTechs offer certain services free of charge. However, customers pay either with data or through attention. With this business model, the idea of offering a premium service in the future can also be pursued, such that customers end up paying in the end. An example of this would be an initially free service that offers regular analysis of the turnover of a current account, with indications of any superfluous subscriptions. The cancellation of a subscription would then be associated with a small fee.

Type 2: Usage-based chargeable service. Here, the end customer pays for individual transactions. An example would be a service in which customers can take out insurance for luggage or a bicycle online in real time.

Type 3: Subscription-based chargeable service. With this variant, end customers regularly pay for the use of a service. This category includes, for example, individual investment advice services, whether automated or not, for which a percentage administration fee per year must be paid.

Type 4: Bilateral analytical service. Here, end customers pay for the evaluation of their data by the FinTech. An example of this is a service in which customers receive an analytical evaluation of their expenses based on location and time.

Type 5: Bilateral personalized transactional service. With this type of business model, users pay for personalized transactions. An example of this would be a service that optimizes a customer's insurance tariffs and also takes over the termination and the new contract.

Type 6: Marketplace paid by business partner. Here, a marketplace is offered on which end customers select their transactions. In the end, the business partner, not the customer, pays for a successful mediation. An example of this would be credit brokerage marketplaces in which the bank that ultimately grants the loan pays a commission to the FinTech.

Type 7: Personalized intermediary paid by counterparties. Here, FinTechs mediate between end customers and the business partner, which ultimately pays for the mediation. The difference between this type and type 6 is that it is not a marketplace, but a product personalized to end customers. An example of this would be a payment service provider that offers mobile payment and charges the merchant a fee, but not the merchant's customers.

Type 8: Nonpersonalized intermediary paid by business partner. As with type 7, the FinTech mediates between end customers and business partners, but the service is not personalized to the customers. An example would be a FinTech that makes paying for a purchase online possible via printed QR codes, which are paid for in the retail trade. The fee is similar to that in type 7, but the process is not personalized to the customers.

While these eight FinTech business model types differ in revenue generation, we assume that though FinTechs often have lower fixed and variable costs than established financial institutions, due to their digitized processes, they must still attract a sufficiently large volume of customer business to stay sustainably profitable. Above all, clear customer benefits must be offered so that FinTechs attain a sufficient number of customers (Dorfleitner et al. 2017a). This can be particularly difficult if the benefits of the service are not immediately obvious or if potential customers do not have sufficient trust in the FinTech. However, the opposite effect can occur as well. For example, Bertsch et al. (2017) show that low confidence in traditional banks has led to high growth in crowdlending. Another possible source of a new customer benefit could come from big data applications, which, as already noted, are currently used by only a few of the FinTech companies.

In the following paragraphs, we conduct a more intensive review of these general considerations for the robo advice subsegment as an example. It should be noted that robo advice FinTechs are most likely to fall under the Type 3 business model. This means that such FinTechs must try to keep their customers permanently to gain sustainable regular payments.

Regarding customer benefits, a recent study on data usage at robo advice FinTechs shows that only part of the data processed from customers is actually used for investment decisions (Tertilt and Scholz 2018). Nevertheless, achievement of a significant customer benefit appears possible if a robo advice FinTech not only provides one-off investment advice but also offers automated asset management. The latter currently corresponds to the majority of robo advisers active in Germany, who also hold a corresponding license as financial portfolio managers in accordance with § 32 of the German Banking Act (*Kreditwesengesetz*). The investor authorizes the robo advice company, as a financial portfolio manager, to manage the portfolio on an ongoing basis within the defined investment guidelines and to rebalance the original portfolio structure automatically in the event of deviations. The automated administration uses algorithms for asset allocation, which are usually based on capital market theory and, in particular, take diversification aspects and a sufficiently high proportion of equities into account. Investors' managed assets, which are often invested in cost-effective exchange-traded funds, are held by the relevant partner bank and are protected in the event of the company's insolvency (BaFin 2016). Although it may seem difficult to beat the market as a whole with such an investment strategy, the generally low fees charged by the corresponding FinTechs allow investors to at least expect to be able to reflect the market in terms of performance.

This, however, would be an important step forward for the many potential customers who have a considerable portion of their assets in their current account without interest or hold them in cash. At the end of the second quarter of 2017, German households held more than 1410 billion euros in cash or demand deposits in bank accounts, which corresponds to almost one-quarter of the total financial assets of private households (Deutsche Bundesbank 2017). Even if only a fraction of this cash is available for longer-term investments, which seems quite realistic, there is already great potential for robo advice. For this reason, we assume that robo advice applications can in principle generate a significant customer benefit.

In this context, we now consider the financial calculation of a robo advice FinTech. The costs of a robo adviser generally include personnel and operating costs. Personnel costs can be estimated at around 92,000 euros per employee per year, if we take into account the personnel costs of German banks and direct banks in the area of investment management (PwC 2016). With an average number of 20 employees,[1] this would result in an expense of 1,840,000 euros per year. According to Moulliet et al. (2016), these personnel costs account for almost 60% of the total expenditure. This means that approximately 1,220,000 euros per year is incurred for operating costs, such as IT and marketing. Overall, the average total costs amount to just under 3 million euros per year. If the robo adviser can earn an annual fee of 0.65% on the assets under management (this corresponds to an average value of the fees of the 14 German robo advisers for assets in the five-digit euro range; see Appendix A.3), approximately 460 million euros are required to cover these total costs. It may be possible to get by with fewer employees in the near future, hiring additional staff only as the company grows, but that does not change the magnitudes much. This means, however, that a robo adviser can work profitably and cover costs in the long run from just under half a billion euros of assets under management. Godenrath (2017) notes that by the end of 2017, such a volume had only been achieved by a single robo adviser in Germany (i.e., Scalable Capital).

It seems realistic that several companies from this subsegment could approach these figures. However, it is doubtful whether any will succeed, especially because there is usually one or more competitors that can offer even more customer benefits than others, so the business is often concentrated with them. In addition, the banks themselves are gradually offering their own robo advice services. In 2017, 3 years after its foundation, the Berlin-based robo adviser Cashboard was already in insolvency.

Thus, we conclude that the business model of a robo adviser FinTech can be sustainably profitable if it creates a corresponding customer benefit and wins the trust of customers. However, the latter is not yet the case (PwC 2016).

In the expert interviews, we asked two questions on the sustainability of the FinTech business models. Figure 5.7 shows the answers to the question whether FinTechs often depend on customer data held by the banks to operate a sustainable

---

[1]This number was determined in mid-2017 via the home pages of 14 robo advisers listed in Appendix A.3.

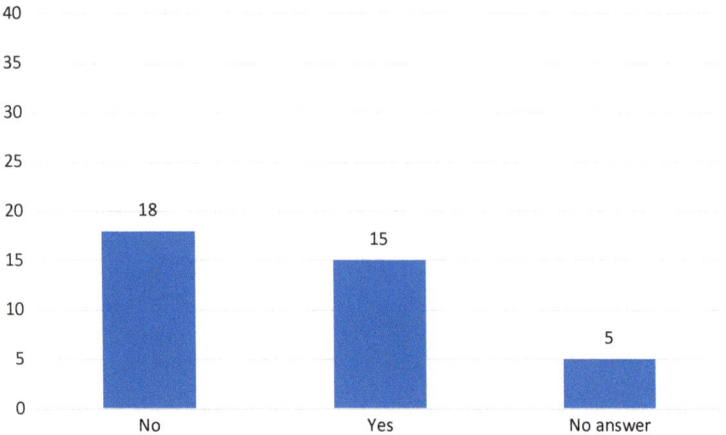

Fig. 5.7 Answers to the question of the dependence of FinTechs on bank customer data

business model (question 12 in Appendix A.2). At 47%, almost half the respondents (18 mentions) answered this question in the negative. FinTechs could also quickly obtain the required data themselves. One respondent said that FinTechs only relied on bank data for their B2B business.

Customer data held at banks are also necessary for cash flow analysis, securities account exchange services, personal financial management, and account information services. Some of the respondents noted that data other than that from the banks (e.g., Amazon.com or Facebook data) would be of greater value to the FinTechs but would usually not be available. Finally, some experts referred to the Second Payment Services Directive, which allows FinTechs to access customer data if customers agree to such access.

In summary, the question whether FinTechs need customer data from banks to operate sustainably at all can be answered in the negative. FinTechs that work with bank customer data in the payment area must be excluded in this context. However, these data are usually voluntarily given to FinTech by customers, or at least the processing is explicitly agreed to, so it cannot be assumed that FinTechs are dependent on banks and the corresponding customer data. This has become especially true since the implementation of the Second Payment Services Directive.

We also raised the question with the experts whether customers' trust or possibly distrust in the established financial institutions plays a role in their choice between FinTechs and banks (question 13 in Appendix A.2). Figure 5.8 shows the answers.

The majority of respondents answered this question in the affirmative (12 mentions). However, the main reasons for using FinTech services are the comparatively lower costs (four mentions) and the simpler handling (three mentions). Six respondents stated that banks had lost the confidence of their customers, especially when it came to investing money. Eleven of the respondents believed that this loss of confidence applied to certain financial services, such as investments, but not to

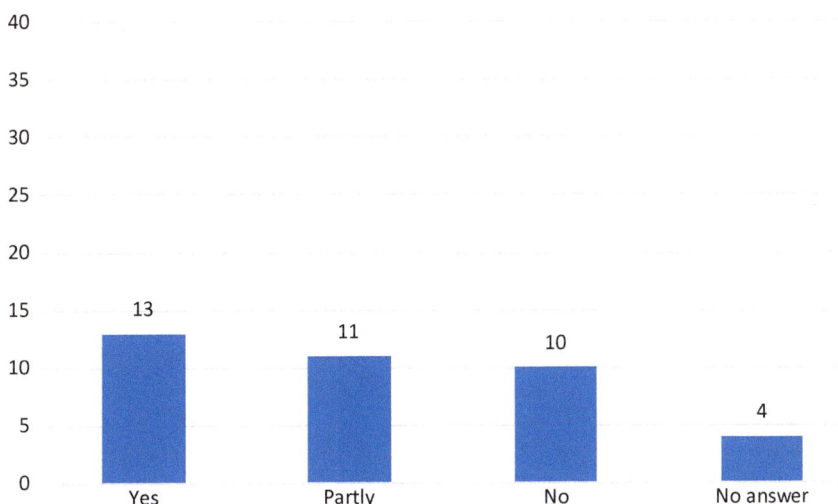

Fig. 5.8   Answers to the question of customers' trust in the established institutions

others, such as payments. Some respondents also noted that this was a generational issue. In the case of the younger generation, a loss of confidence in banks would have come after the financial crisis due to, for example, incorrect advice and nontransparent commission payments. In summary, many arguments are in favor of the thesis that the decision for or against a FinTech is also a question of trust. In addition, this trust is likely dependent on the particular service and the age of the relevant customer.

With regard to the sustainability of the business models, it generally depends on the extent to which FinTechs can first generate additional customer benefits and then can give customers a sense of trustworthiness. If so, sustainable business activity is possible with many FinTech models. Without doubt, however, many FinTechs will leave the market because their business models do not convince their customers or are too similar to a better-positioned competitor. This is a natural phenomenon for start-up companies.

A strong dependence of the sustainability of business models on customer data held by banks can also not be ascertained. However, cooperation with banks helps many FinTechs grow faster, as banks already have a large customer base from which FinTechs can draw. An example of this is the cooperation between the robo adviser Scalable Capital and ING-DiBa, which has led to the rapid increase in assets under management (Godenrath 2017). Ultimately, such cooperation is accompanied by a transfer of trust from the bank to the FinTech. From the banks' perspective, this again suggests that they should try to offer their own FinTech products in the long run.

5.4 FinTechs with a Debt Capital Focus

An important question in the context of FinTechs is whether the offerings of the new digital players create a change in the economic situation such that customers gain access to the market through access to loans and loan substitutes. First, it is clear that some relevant FinTechs on the market are offering loans and/or loan substitutes. Several financing platforms act as credit intermediaries and/or pawnbrokers for small and medium-sized enterprises. Some factoring FinTechs (Dorfleitner and Rad 2017) and marketplace lending platforms also focus explicitly on the financing for small and medium-sized enterprises. Examples are the offers of auxmoney, Compeon, creditshelf, Funding Circle, Rechnung48, and Valendo. The issuance of newly created own cryptoassets, so-called initial coin offerings, are frequently debt capital–like forms of financing, which are suitable only for few companies.

It should be noted that some companies in Germany have poor access to debt capital (Lopez de Silanes et al. 2015). These are often small companies without Basel II-compliant collateral that require comparatively small loan amounts, so traditional credit processing, including solvency assessment, is not worthwhile for a traditional bank. One respondent estimated that in Germany, approximately 10% of industries (*Gewerbe*) effectively have no access to bank loans. Some FinTech companies operate corresponding platforms and have identified these small companies as a target group. How sustainable each individual FinTech is in this area cannot be conclusively analyzed in the context of this book. However, customer benefits for professionals and the self-employed, who are otherwise cut off from loans and credit substitutes, can be assumed.

Even if these customers have high default rates, which is not necessarily the case, because the high fixed costs of the banks are often the reason for not granting the loan and not bad credit ratings, this may not be problematic for FinTechs. That is, FinTechs can reduce transaction costs by digitizing numerous processes and otherwise demand risk-adequate interest rates and build on the diversification of those that ultimately assume the credit risk. This is shown in the analysis of the credit marketplaces auxmoney and Smava by Dorfleitner et al. (2016) or the world's largest online factoring market (Dorfleitner et al. 2017b). Comparatively high interest rates do not need to be a problem for the borrower. If a relatively small loan is required and the associated purchase quickly amortizes, which is easily possible with smaller companies because they have more growth potential, the question of which interest rate exactly must be paid does not play a major role for the company.[2] This effect is already known from microloans (Dorfleitner et al. 2013).

---

[2]For example, consider a fictitious graphic designer who, to obtain interesting orders, needs a high-quality computer for 5000 euros. He does not have the financial means to purchase the computer outright, so he needs a loan. Already with the first order, he can earn 6000 euros contribution margin within half a year. If he now pays 10% interest p.a., he will incur a cost of 250 euros, whereas at an interest rate of 6%, he would only pay 150 euros. The additional cost of 100 euros is hardly significant for him because it is almost negligible in relation to the return on the purchase. Given the alternative of not securing the loan from a traditional bank, he thus could even afford significantly higher interest rates.

Finally, risks could also arise in this context if, for example, loans were securitized on a large scale. Although this can have positive effects on liquidity and, thus, the growth of these markets, it could also give rise to systemic risks if mainly loans with poor risks are securitized (Dorfleitner et al. 2017a, p. 99). As is well known, such an approach in connection with US subprime loans led to the financial crisis of 2008–2009. This approach would also have adverse effects if the new actors were to grant loans that were not worthy of financing on a larger scale. However, the question again would be who would assume the credit risk. Only if many of these risks converged and were also financed with a great amount of borrowed capital could serious dangers for the economy arise. At present, this is not indicated by the low overall volume (Dorfleitner et al. 2019).

In the context of this topic, the experts were also asked whether some FinTechs would consciously target customers and companies with their products and services that would have difficulty obtaining outside capital in the banking system. All respondents answered this question in the affirmative. Some platforms, such as auxmoney, would have attracted bad debtors in the first place. However, this would no longer be the case. By using big data and AI, it may be possible to grant loans here that banks would not have granted, even though the debtors would probably have repaid. Some of these FinTech companies had trained their models with data in Poland and the Ukraine.

In summary, in the area of debt capital focused FinTechs, the debt capital market has expanded and is also accompanied by a certain economic added value, albeit to a limited extent. Nevertheless, further developments should be monitored with regard to undesirable developments, such as the systematic securitization of bad loans.

References

Bachmann, R., Kemper, G., & Gerzer, T. (2014). *Big Data—Fluch oder Segen?* Heidelberg: mitp.

BaFin (2016). *Automatisierte Finanzportfolioverwaltung.* Retrieved from https://www.bafin.de/DE/Aufsicht/FinTech/Finanzportfolioverwaltung/finanzportfolioverwaltung_node.html

Baron, P. (2013). *Big Data für IT-Entscheider: Riesige Datenmengen und moderne Technologien gewinnbringend nutzen.* Munich: Hanser.

Bertsch, C., Hull, I., Qi, Y., & Zhang, X. (2017). *The role of trust in online lending.* Sveriges Riksbank working paper series Nr. 346.

Brandl, B., & Hornuf, L. (2017). *Where did FinTechs come from, and where do they go? The transformation of the financial industry in Germany after digitalization.* SSRN Working Paper. Retrieved from https://ssrn.com/abstract=3036555

Buchanan, J. M. (1989). *Liberty, market and state: Political economy in the 1980s.* New York: New York University Press.

Chamoni, P., & Gluchowski, P. (2017). Business analytics—State of the art. *Controlling and Management Review, 61*(4), 8–17.

Coase, R. H. (1960). The problem of social cost. *Journal of Law and Economics, 3,* 1–44.

Dapp, T.-F. (2015). *Fintech reloaded—Traditional banks as digital ecosystems: With proven walled garden strategies into the future.* Frankfurt am Main: Deutsche Bank Research.

Deutsche Bundesbank (2017). *Geldvermögensbildung und Außenfinanzierung in Deutschland im zweiten Quartal 2017: Geldvermögen und Verbindlichkeiten (unkonsolidiert).* Retrieved from https://www.bundesbank.de/Redaktion/DE/Pressemitteilungen/BBK/2017/2017_10_13_ geldvermoegen_bestaende.pdf?__blob=publicationFile

Dorfleitner, G., & Rad, J. (2017). Wie FinTechs den Factoring-Markt neu gestalten. *Corporate Finance, 2017,* 358–363.

Dorfleitner, G., Leidl, M., Priberny, C., & von Mosch, J. (2013). What determines microcredit interest rates? *Applied Financial Economics, 23*(20), 1579–1597.

Dorfleitner, G., Priberny, C., Schuster, S., Stoiber, J., Weber, M., de Castro, I., & Kammler, J. (2016). Description-text related soft information in peer-to-peer lending—Evidence from two leading European platforms. *Journal of Banking and Finance, 64,* 169–187.

Dorfleitner, G., Hornuf, L., Schmitt, M., & Weber, M. (2017a). *FinTech in Germany.* Cham: Springer International.

Dorfleitner, G., Rad, J., & Weber, M. (2017b). Pricing in the online invoice trading market: First empirical evidence. *Economics Letters, 161,* 56–61.

Dorfleitner, G., Hornuf, L., Schmitt, M., & Weber, M. (2019). Marktüberblick. In F. Möslein & S. Omlor (Eds.), *FinTech-Handbuch. Digitalisierung, Recht, Finanzen* (pp. 21–38). Munich: C.H.Beck.

Eck, W. A. (2017). Informationen rücken näher zusammen. *Bankmagazin, 2017*(7–8), 50–53.

Frien, B. (2017). *Gegner, Helfer, Partner: Fintechs und das Firmenkundengeschäft der Banken.* Frankfurt am Main: Frankfurt Business Media.

Gimpel, H., Rau, D., & Röglinger, M. (2016). FinTech-Geschäftsmodelle im Visier. *Wirtschaftsinformatik & Management, 2016*(3), 38–47.

Godenrath, B. (2017). Robo-Rugby. *Börsen-Zeitung of December 30th, 2017,* 34.

Hornuf, L. Klus, M. F., Lohwasser, T. S., & Schwienbacher, A. (2018). *How do banks interact with FinTechs? Forms of alliances and their impact on bank value.* SSRN Working Paper. Retrieved from https://www.ssrn.com/abstract=3252318

Lerner, J., Baker, M., Speen, A., & Leamon, A. (2015). Financial patent quality: Finance patents after State Street. *Havard Business School Working Paper,* 16–068.

Lopez de Silanes, F., McCahery, J., Schoenmaker, D., & Stanisic, D. (2015). *The European capital markets study: Estimating the financing gaps of SMEs.* Amsterdam: Duisenberg School of Finance.

Moulliet, D., Stolzenbach, J., Bein, A., & Wagner, I. (2016). *Cost-income ratios and robo-advisory: Why wealth managers need to engage with robo-advisors.* Deloitte. Retrieved from https://www2.deloitte.com/content/dam/Deloitte/de/Documents/financial-services/Robo-Advisory-in-Wealth-Management.pdf

PwC (2016). *Wie profitabel ist das Privatkundengeschäft in Deutschland?* Retrieved from https://www.pwc.de/de/finanzdienstleistungen/assets/pwc-wie-profitabel-ist-das-privatkundengeschaeft-in-deutschland-2016.pdf

Schwarz, T. (2015). *Big Data im Marketing: Chancen und Möglichkeiten für eine effektive Kundenansprache.* Munich: Haufe Lexware Verlag.

Teece, D. J. (1986). Profiting from technological innovation: Implications for integration, collaboration, licensing and public policy. *Research Policy, 15*(6), 285–305.

Teece, D. J. (1998). Capturing value from knowledge assets: The new economy, markets for know-how, and intangible assets. *California Management Review, 40*(3), 55–79.

Tertilt, M., & Scholz, P. (2018). To advise, or not to advise—How robo-advisors evaluate the risk preferences of private investors. *Journal of Wealth Management, 21*(2), 70–84.

Yan, J., Yu, W., & Zhao, J. L. (2015). How signaling and search costs affect information asymmetry in P2P lending: The economics of big data. *Financial Innovation, 1*(1), 19e.

Zetzsche, D. A., Buckley, R., Arner, D., & Barberis, J. N. (2018). From FinTech to TechFin: The regulatory challenges of data-driven inance. *NYU Journal of Law and Business, 14*(2), 393–446.

Chapter 6
Need For Regulation in the German FinTech Market

Abstract This chapter analyzes the potential need for regulation in the German FinTech market. To this end, theoretical considerations and insights from expert interviews are discussed. Both our theoretical findings and the expert interviews suggest that further regulation of many details around FinTechs is necessary and that this particularly applies to aspects of data protection and data sovereignty, as well as to the need for legislation and supervisory authorities to keep pace with technological developments.

Whether further regulation of the content of privacy statements is necessary cannot be clarified within the framework of this book and is left to the judgment of legal investigations. However, it is clear that the GDPR and also the planned ePrivacy Regulation, which replaces the Directive on Electronic Communications (2002/58/EG) and the so-called Cookie Directive (2009/136/EG), have strengthened and will strengthen the de lege lata rights of users of FinTech services. It is questionable, however, whether users will actually gain more sovereignty over their data. In reality, users of FinTech services must agree to the processing of personal data to be able to make use of FinTech services. The consent of users, however, often represents a universal solution for the legally compliant processing of personal data for FinTech companies. Moreover, usually only a few users are likely to read the privacy statements (Ben-Shahar and Schneider 2014), as in most cases the customer benefit and the price of the service are the main factors in a consumer's decision. If the processing of certain personal data widely occurs in the FinTech industry and the privacy statements are not read, the requirement for online merchants to offer different payment services is of little benefit. In this sense, the recent ruling of the German Federal Supreme Court (dated 18.07.2017, file no. KZR 39/16), which prohibits online merchants such as Deutsche Bahn from offering the payment service sofortüberweisung.de as the only free means of payment, also means nothing.

Especially if a great deal of data are processed, FinTechs must also be able to create extensive privacy statements. However, this should not be at the expense of the legibility and comprehensibility of the privacy statements. To make the relevant information easily understandable for users, such as what data are passed on to whom, the privacy statements should be prepared in a standardized way as far as

© Springer Nature Switzerland AG 2019   107
G. Dorfleitner, L. Hornuf, *FinTech and Data Privacy in Germany*,
https://doi.org/10.1007/978-3-030-31335-7_6

possible and relevant information should be provided. It does not seem evident that such standardization requires legislative steps. Rather, an industry code of conduct and/or a corresponding model privacy statement could achieve this goal. If legislative intervention is required at all, this could be done through information and training measures on data protection issues. More transparency and comparability of the data processed by different FinTech companies would also be desirable, possibly leading to not only price competition but also contract design and data minimization competition. At the same time, violations of data protection or weaknesses in data security should not have to be identified and followed up by users but by appropriate supervisory authorities, such as federal and state data protection commissioners. However, they are already implementing appropriate measures today.

In November 2017, the FinTech Council of the German Federal Ministry of Finance contributed to the debate on the further regulation of FinTechs with a position paper containing several reform proposals (FinTechRat 2017). In addition to some demands that directly affect government action, such as facilitating the immigration of IT specialists, greater expenditure on infrastructure and education, and the targeted piloting of new technologies, it contains suggestions and proposals for regulatory needs in the following six areas:

1. *Establishment of clear principles for legislation as a prerequisite for successful digitalization*: At the heart of this is the demand to formulate laws and regulatory standards in such a way that companies wishing to use a particular digital innovation are not disadvantaged. The written form requirement is cited as an example, which discriminates against innovative solutions under certain circumstances.

2. *Identification and anti-money-laundering requirements, customer communication, and contracting*: This requirement refers to the possibility of multiple uses of customer identification data collected once, which would simplify the handling of offers for customers, but is currently not possible because of anti-money-laundering requirements.

3. *Extension of the regulatory framework to providers of critical infrastructure, in particular cloud services*: The requirement stipulates that if financial service companies use infrastructure services, in particular cloud services, from other companies, these service providers must also possess a corresponding new license to be created.

4. *Strengthening IT competence in management*: This proposal suggests that companies, be they FinTechs or established financial institutions that offer IT-based services on a larger scale, also require corresponding IT competence in management.

5. *Definition of data sovereignty*: This aspect represents the demand for the formulation of various legal norms with the aim to enable citizens to freely decide what data they share with which providers and, in doing so, regain sovereignty over their data.

6. *Regulatory framework for deep learning or AI*: The aim of this requirement is to create a regulatory framework for the applications of AI and deep learning, which then permits, restricts, or prohibits the use of certain procedures in certain contexts.

These regulatory demands of the FinTech Council go far beyond the mere application to FinTechs and concern all kinds of mobile and web-based services. In principle, the demands appear to be reasonable and relevant. The aforementioned findings of this book on the sustainability of business models tend to underscore requirement 1, our findings on big data applications underscore requirement 6, and our comprehensive analysis of data protection aspects underscores requirements 3 and 5.

The FinTech Council does not explicitly call for a regulatory sandbox regulation for FinTechs, as already established in some other countries (Anand and Shah 2017; FinTechRat 2017; Zetzsche et al. 2017). In addition, according to our findings, a regulatory sandbox for German FinTechs as a whole does not seem recommendable. On the one hand, start-up companies must first overcome fixed costs, which can sometimes be higher in the financial sector. On the other hand, these fixed costs can also be reduced through clear rules tailored to the requirements of digitization within the existing legal framework. In addition, a service-oriented financial supervisory authority can support FinTech companies in developing their business models. In the case of a sandbox solution, it could otherwise be the case that only a few innovative FinTechs would choose a sandbox exception and the most promising FinTechs a full regulation immediately (Dorfleitner et al. 2017, p. 99).

The expert interviews also included questions on regulatory aspects. Figure 6.1 shows the answers to the question whether there is a need for specific regulation tailored to FinTechs (question 5 in Appendix A.2).

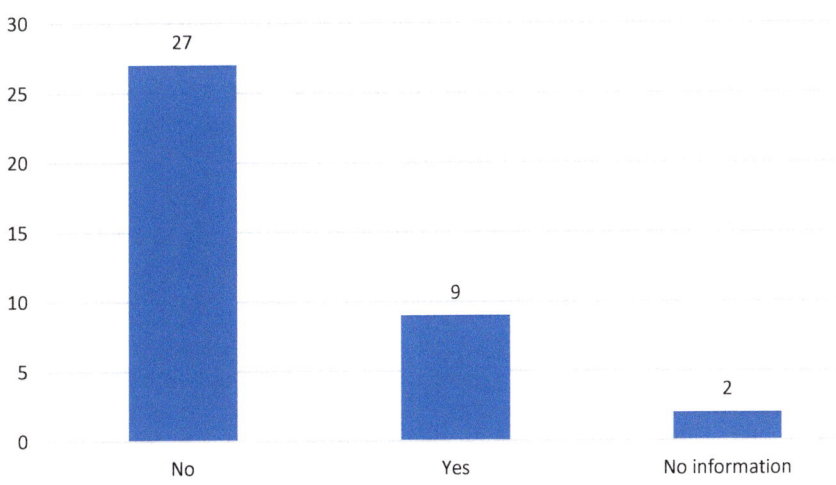

Fig. 6.1 Answers to the question regarding a specific regulation tailored to FinTechs

About one-quarter of the respondents believed that there was a need for specific regulation (nine mentions). At 71%, however, the majority of respondents (27 mentions) rejected this. Some experts also stated that the legislator only had to subsume the technology under existing law. In this context, some respondents argued that the "same business, same risk, same regulation" rule should apply, as this would ensure the primacy of equal competitive conditions for all market participants.

Some respondents noted that a specific FinTech regulation should be in favor of new market participants in the financial services sector with the need to overcome high fixed costs to enter the market (five mentions). High fixed costs would put a disproportionate burden on small companies, and these barriers to market entry would prevent innovation and competition. For this reason, small companies in particular would need to be promoted by regulatory exceptions. A possible solution to make it easier for these companies to enter the market is a regulatory sandbox (six mentions). The following further arguments were mentioned in this context:

- High barriers to market entry also sometimes mean that FinTech business models have a circumventing character. API banking is an example of this. Some banks would not exist without FinTech B2B customers.
- The fact that no large digital ecosystem or TechFin comes from Europe would prove that the barriers to market entry for small, innovative companies were too high.
- Small businesses also would benefit from legal exemptions in other areas. Examples of this are labor law (e.g., the simplified dismissal of employees), consumer law (e.g., the control of general terms and conditions, the concept of entrepreneur), accounting law, tax law, and antitrust law. Consequently, there could also be corresponding exceptions in banking law.
- In some countries, therefore, a level system of regulation would prevail in banking law, which regulates FinTechs to different extents depending on the financial volume and the type of financial transactions carried out.
- This raises the question of how far a regulatory sandbox should be defined and which regulatory facts should be subject to an exception. A regulatory sandbox has already been implemented in England, Singapore, and Switzerland.
- As an alternative to a regulatory sandbox, some respondents from the German supervisory side stressed that the supervisory authority could also support FinTechs in their business models.

However, many respondents who rejected specific FinTech regulation suggested that digital financial services generally needed specific regulation, regardless of who provided them. In this context, the following arguments were presented:

- Certain developments in the FinTech area cannot be subsumed under current legislation. Blockchain-based investments, for example, might not be controllable with the existing instruments of capital market law, as they could be designed in such a way that they are either financial instruments or not.
- Customers must be able to regain sovereignty over their data.

- As another argument in favor of FinTech-specific regulation, a level playing field must be created for technology-driven companies. For example, the written form requirement makes many developments difficult in the digital world. Any FinTech regulation must, therefore, be technology neutral and technology open. For example, there is no regulation when investment data are preselected manually, only when this is automated and digital.

Figure 6.2 shows the answers to the question whether supervision by BaFin or the German Trade Regulation Act (*Gewerbeordnung*—GewO) leads to a systematic distortion of competition between banks and FinTechs (question 6 in Appendix A.2). The interviewees were not united on this question; five did not want to answer it at all, 15 affirmed the question, and 18 denied it. It has often been argued that while banks and FinTechs would not be regulated differently for the same business, FinTechs would define and develop their business model in such a way that they would not be subject to BaFin supervision. FinTechs would select the transactions such that BaFin supervision could be avoided because the fixed costs associated with this would be too high. One reason for the regulatory separation would be that FinTechs deliberately only carried out certain transactions and thus did not fall under BaFin supervision. By contrast, banks are generally supervised by BaFin, given the diversity and scope of their own business. The Trade Regulation Act is significantly less strict than BaFin supervision. As a result, banks would be subject to higher scrutiny.

A consequence of the BaFin supervision is that one must know one's own banking systems very well. The problem is that, for example, in an ECB audit, the technical terms must also be understood in English.

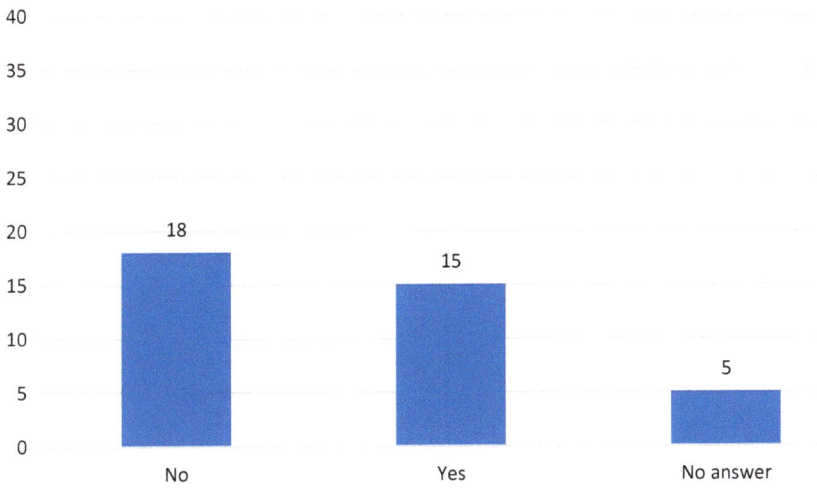

Fig. 6.2 Answers to the question regarding a distortion of competition through supervision by BaFin vs. German Commercial Code

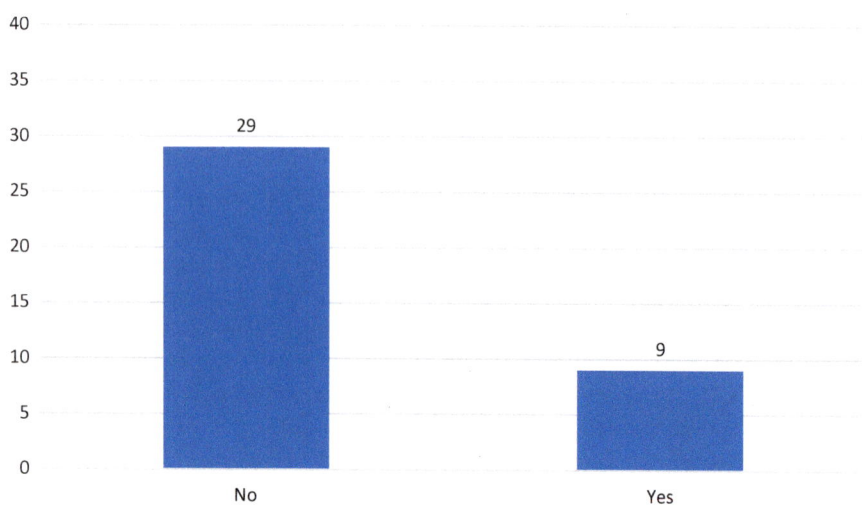

Fig. 6.3 Answers to the question regarding a different regulation for FinTechs and banks

Equity crowdfunding and robo advice were cited as examples of unequal treatment.

- Equity crowdfunding portals in Germany are subject to the Trade Regulation Act and in France, for example, to the Financial Market Supervisory Authority.
- Robo advice companies in Germany often operate without a banking license, though some of the surveyed legal experts believed that this is necessary.

The differences in the exemptions were also particularly relevant to the respondents. For example, an exemption from the prospectus requirement of up to 100,000 euros[1] applies to securities, while exceptions of up to 2,500,000 million euros apply to investments (*Vermögensanlagen*). It was suggested that FinTech companies should at least report to BaFin so that it can keep track of the market. Similar requirements exist, for example, for equity crowdfunding portals and companies in France and Italy. It was also questioned whether banks could set up FinTech start-ups that would benefit from the same exceptions or whether these would then be fully regulated.

Finally, Fig. 6.3 shows the answers to the question whether banks and FinTechs are regulated differently for the same business activity (question 6 in Appendix A.2).

While more than half the respondents said "yes" to the question whether supervision by BaFin or trade supervisory authorities leads to a distortion of competition between FinTechs and banks, less than one-third (nine mentions) stated that banks and FinTechs were regulated differently for the same business activity. According to some respondents, this is because FinTechs are adjusting their business models

---

[1]In the meantime, the value for the exception from the obligation to publish a prospectus for securities is 8 million euros.

accordingly, so as not to be subject to BaFin supervision. The decisive factor was that the regulation was linked to activities and transactions (i.e., companies that carry out certain activities) and not to the size or business models of the companies.

Differences in regulation were mentioned in particular in the following areas:

- Most frequently mentioned was the unequal regulation between banks and account information service providers or payment initiation service providers, but this had largely been abolished with the introduction and implementation of the Second Payment Services Directive (five mentions).
- Furthermore, differences in the area of data protection and data security exist between banks and FinTechs. The systems of the banks would need to meet stricter requirements, and the customer data would be largely unprotected at FinTechs. FinTechs often do not have redundant systems, as banks do.
- The verity risk is more pronounced at FinTechs. A bank must prove that a customer had a claim and against whom. In equity crowdfunding, this is often not known. A copy of a contract is not sufficient. The bank would need to identify the buyer and be able to assess the end customer. To do so, IT systems would be needed, as would balance sheets of the person who buys (e.g., an articulated lorry).
- Differences also exist in the requirements of the compliance, in the personal nature of the identification, and with anti-money-laundering topics.
- There is now regulatory competition for sometimes laxer locations for a particular activity. The Swiss supervisory authority, for example, makes great efforts not to regard initial coin offerings as securities to locate them in Switzerland. In the case of other activities that are still in test status or are to be politically promoted, the regulatory authorities might turn a blind eye in some places. An example of this "benevolent" regulation is the Crypto Valley in the Swiss canton of Zug (https:// cryptovalley.swiss). It is also important that law enforcement at banks and FinTechs be handled in the same way. However, initial coin offerings have been treated more laxly so far. Particularly with these offerings, some FinTechs are not even aware that they were regulated.

Overall, we note that there are indications of minor regulatory benefits for FinTechs. However, FinTechs may also experience disadvantages from unequal regulation. The Regulatory Technical Standards presented by the European Banking Authority for the implementation of the Second Payment Services Directive can serve as an example (European Banking Authority 2017). There is certain unequal treatment here because banks, but not the FinTechs, are allowed to define the standards for interfaces (see also Haddad and Hornuf 2019).

In summary, both our own findings and the expert interviews, as well as the demands of the FinTech Council, provide a clear picture: further regulation of many details around FinTechs appears necessary. This applies particularly to aspects of data protection and data sovereignty, but there is also the need for legislation and supervisory authorities to keep pace with technological developments.

References

Anand, V., & Shah, S. (2017). *Regulatory sandbox: Making India a global FinTech hub*. Gurgaon: Deloitte.

Ben-Shahar, O., & Schneider, C. (2014). *More than you wanted to know: The failure of mandated disclosure*. Princeton: Princeton University Press.

Dorfleitner, G., Hornuf, L., Schmitt, M., & Weber, M. (2017). *FinTech in Germany*. Cham: Springer International.

European Banking Authority (2017). *Final report: Draft regulatory technical standards on strong customer authentication and common and secure communication under article 98 of Directive 2015/2366 (PSD2)*. Retrieved from https://www.eba.europa.eu/documents/10180/1761863/Final+draft+RTS+on+SCA+and+CSC+under+PSD2+%28EBA-RTS-2017-02%29.pdf

FinTechRat (2017). *Reformvorschläge von Mitgliedern des FinTechRats*. Retrieved from http://www.bundesfinanzministerium.de/Content/DE/Standardartikel/Themen/Schlaglichter/Fintech/2017-12-01-Fintech-Reformvorschlaege-Download.pdf?__blob=publicationFile&v=1

Haddad, C., & Hornuf, L. (2019). The emergence of the global FinTech market: Economic and technological determinants. *Small Business Economics, 53*(1), 81–105.

Zetzsche, D. A., Buckley, R. P., Barberis, J. N., & Arner, D. W. (2017). Regulating a revolution: From regulatory sandboxes to smart regulation. *Fordham Journal of Corporate and Financial Law, 23*(1), 31–103.

Chapter 7
Summary in Eleven Theses

Abstract The chapter summarizes the results of this book in the form of eleven theses. The theses are based on the evaluation of the privacy statements of FinTechs operating in Germany, the evaluation of 36 expert interviews, and the theoretical and empirical arguments presented in the previous chapters. They provide pointed statements for discussions on the future of the FinTech sector and on practical and policy implications in the field of FinTech and the usage of data.

We summarize the results of this book in the form of 11 theses, based on the privacy statements of FinTechs operating in Germany, the expert interviews, and the theoretical and empirical arguments presented in the previous chapters. Therefore, the theses are no longer substantiated in detail here, but only briefly described.

Thesis 1: Regulation specifically for FinTechs makes little sense, while adaptation of existing regulations to the digitization of financial services would be appropriate.

Although a sandbox solution has been requested by some FinTech representatives, it does not appear necessary after weighing all aspects. In addition, several aspects in the context of digital financial services require more precise regulation. For example, there is a demand to adapt the current rules quickly and at regular intervals to technical progress. In addition, some FinTech companies are currently experiencing problems with existing regulatory requirements not being adequately monitored, such as the clever circumvention of certain licensing requirements.

Thesis 2: Big data currently plays a certain role in the FinTech sector but, in most cases, not a very large one.

There are undoubtedly various applications of big data in the FinTech sector. However, only a few FinTechs use them in such a way that they are a critical part of the business model. One possible reason for this is that traditional financial data are already meaningful for many business models. Many FinTechs do not use big data analytics at all, though a few use big data applications, such as a credit-scoring model based on big data as a basic component of their business model. These firms are based in Germany but mainly grant loans abroad.

© Springer Nature Switzerland AG 2019

G. Dorfleitner, L. Hornuf, *FinTech and Data Privacy in Germany*,

https://doi.org/10.1007/978-3-030-31335-7_7

Thesis 3: Almost all German FinTechs process data on their users to a certain extent, and though this is explicitly mentioned in privacy statements, users often have to accept the privacy policy in order to use the FinTech service.

A large proportion of FinTechs process personal data, and most provide this information in privacy statements. The majority also share personal data with third parties. At the same time, many FinTechs are unclear about the customer benefits that can be gained from processing these data, in the sense of big data application, for example. However, most customers are confronted with the problem of having to accept the privacy policy in order to use the FinTech offer. There are indications that many users do not read the privacy statements in detail.

Thesis 4: In the majority of cases, the privacy statements drawn up by the FinTech companies do not conclusively state what data are processed and to whom they are forwarded.

The GDPR, which became binding in 2018, stipulates that information on the processing of personal user data is to be provided in a comprehensible manner. The FinTech companies, however, seldom state conclusively in their privacy statements what data are processed and to whom the data are shared. FinTech companies often limit themselves to examples or a legal definition of what personal data are. As the processed data is quite extensive in some cases and the privacy statement can become very long with a final listing, standardization could help with the representation of the information.

Thesis 5: The processing of personal data by third parties should be made transparent and conclusive by the FinTech companies.

When using the services of third parties, FinTech companies often state that they cannot prevent the processing of data by third parties or cannot precisely determine the data processed by third parties. Instead, reference is made to the information on the websites of the respective third parties. This approach requires a major effort from users, as some companies use up to 19 web tracking and advertising services and also integrate social plug-ins. A more economical and efficient solution would be for the FinTech companies to list the data processed by third parties for users, rather than forcing each user to find out for him- or herself which third-party services are being used and what data are being processed in which way.

Thesis 6: A comparison of the privacy statements before and after the GDPR became binding shows that data protection has often not improved and, in some cases, has even developed to the disadvantage of the data subjects. Consumer associations could play an important role in enforcement.

Some FinTechs that initially had no privacy statements developed one after the GDPR became binding. The FinTech companies that already had a privacy statement before the GDPR became binding adapted it in four of five cases. This adaptation was accompanied by two general trends: first, privacy statements are now more than twice as comprehensive as before, and second, they now consist more of standardized text modules. As a consequence of the latter trend, in many areas of the statements, it is less frequently stated exhaustively what personal data are processed, what personal data are passed on to third parties, and who these third parties are. A conclusive list of this information would make it necessary to prepare the privacy statements in an individualized and nonstandardized way. FinTechs are often asked, on the one hand, to inform their users completely, but on the other hand, to inform users only briefly and concisely. It may be that only professional players can enforce the rights of numerous customers, for which the costs of enforcement are usually too high. Consumer protection associations in particular are under obligation here, and they should also be given sufficient human and financial resources to enforce the rights.

Thesis 7: Cooperation between banks and FinTechs creates added value, at least for these two parties but usually for customers as well.

From a theoretical standpoint, this insight is initially trivial, as cooperation should only come about if both sides profit from it. In practice, however, cooperation can also fail because the added value does not arise to the extent it was expected. In addition, from the banks' point of view, some cooperation must be considered against the background that they may have to accept the loss of previous advantages or economic rents. An example would be cooperation with a robo advice FinTech, which may entice wealthy customers whose investment advice has so far earned more than the commission paid by the robo adviser away from the bank.

Thesis 8: FinTechs are dependent not on the customer data processed by banks to operate a sustainable business model but, instead, on offering their customers sustainable added value.

Certain customer data held by banks are absolutely necessary for some FinTechs in the payment area to carry out their services. This was also noted by some experts. However, data are either voluntarily passed on to FinTechs by customers themselves or must be passed on by banks within the framework of the Second Payment Services Directive following the consent of customers. Nevertheless, it can be assumed that the business models of many FinTechs will not function sustainably because the customer benefit is not perceived as sufficiently large. Some of the FinTechs founded a few years ago have already ceased business activities.

Thesis 9: In the long run, there will no longer be the established financial institutions on one side and FinTechs as opponents on the other side; instead, different financial services will be offered by a multitude of players.

Already today there are fixed cooperations between FinTechs and banks, and some successful FinTechs have become banks themselves. Banks now also offer FinTech services, such as instant payment functions or robo advice. Many FinTechs will fail, but some will maintain their business and grow. New FinTechs may continue to appear on the market. In addition, large digital companies such as Alibaba, Amazon.com, Apple, Facebook, Google, and Tencent are gradually entering the FinTech market. In the end, they too may act like a bank or an established

FinTech. All in all, there will be many digital financial services offered by young or established companies from the financial or technology sector that operate under a banking and/or asset management license or, if necessary, only broker banking services via API banking.

Thesis 10: FinTechs can provide private individuals or small companies with additional access to debt capital.

Some FinTechs specialize in offering loans and credit substitutes to individuals and companies that otherwise have poor access to debt. This may lead to an efficient expansion of the debt capital market, which is also expected to generate added economic value, but is still limited in scope. This development should nevertheless be considered with regard to undesirable developments, especially when institutional investors enter the market and loans are securitized in nontransparent procedures.

Thesis 11: Banks still often enjoy greater customer confidence than FinTechs. However, this depends on the age of the customers and the respective financial services and is likely to decrease over time.

The customer confidence that banks enjoy was relatively clear from the expert survey. Trust in banks and FinTechs appears to be age dependent though, with older people putting greater trust in banks than younger people, especially digital natives. Therefore, it is only a matter of time before the majority of users switch over to FinTechs or TechFins, unless banks take appropriate countermeasures.

Appendix A

A.1 List of Experts

Adelt, Marco, Dr. (CEO, Clark)

Bajorat, André Marseille (CEO, figo)

Bartz, Chris (CEO & Co-Founder, Elinvar)

Bertsch, Christoph, PhD (Research Division, Swedish central bank)

Böringschulte, Kai (CEO & Founder, Compeon)

Conreder, Christian, Dr. (Associate Partner, Rödl & Partner)

Dautzenberg, Kirsti, Dr. (Team Leader Marktwächter Digitale Welt, Federal Consumers' Association)

Dietze, Doris (Head of Unit, Digital Finance Technologies, Payments, and Financial Sanctions (VIIA3b), Federal Ministry of Finance)

Eichler, Carolyn (Legal Officer at the Berlin Commissioner for Data Protection and Freedom of Information)

Fiedler, Ingo, Dr. (Research Director Blockchain Research Lab, University of Hamburg)

Heist, Alexander (N.N.)

Kempf, Stefan (CEO, Elbe Finanzgruppe)

Kladny, Timo (CEO, betterplace.org)

Klein, Gerald (CEO & Founder, growney)

Klöhn, Lars, Prof. Dr. (Humboldt University of Berlin)

Leichsenring, Hansjörg, Dr. (Business Consultant and Interim Manager, Der Bank-Blog)

Mayer-Wanders, Ursula (Federal Financial Supervisory Authority—BaFin)

Möslein, Florian, Prof. Dr. (University of Marburg)

Moukabary, Gamal, Dr. (CEO, Co-founder, bonify)

N.N. (Team Leader Internet Solutions of a major German bank)

Natusch, Ingo, Dr. (Head of Department PBK Audit and Advisory Company for the Banking Industry, Audit Association of German Banks)

© Springer Nature Switzerland AG 2019

G. Dorfleitner, L. Hornuf, *FinTech and Data Privacy in Germany*,

https://doi.org/10.1007/978-3-030-31335-7

Nießner, Stefan (Banking Supervision, Deutsche Bundesbank)
Oehler, Andreas, Prof. Dr. (University of Bamberg)
Omlor, Sebastian, Prof. Dr. (University of Marburg)
Penzel, Hans-Gert, Prof. Dr. (CEO, ibi research at the University of Regensburg)
Pöschl, Patrick (Co-founder, Scalable Capital)
Puschmann, Thomas, Dr. (Head, Swiss FinTech Innovation Lab)
Rathmann, Birgit (General Manager, Customer Service, VR-NetWorld)
Röder, Roland, Dr. (Vertriebsleiter & Direktor, Frankfurter Sparkasse)
Sandler, Guido, Dr. (CEO, Bergfürst)
Schmütsch, Jan Peter, Dr. (Project Manager, Boston Consulting Group)
Schobert, Franziska, Dr. (Division Markets, Policy Issues of Monetary Policy
    Instruments, Deutsche Bundesbank)
Scholz, Peter, Prof. Dr. (Hamburg School of Business Administration)
Schulz, Sebastian (Head of Legal Policy & Data Protection, Federal Association of
    German E-Commerce and Mail Order Business e.V.)
Stavreva, Nevena (Head of Business Development, eCollect)
Thielmann, Sebastian (Head of Strategy and Policy, Ostsächsische Sparkasse
    Dresden)
von Berenberg-Consbruch, John (CEO, Valendo)
Wendelberger, Christoph (Group Leader Projects & Processes, ebase)
Winter, Heike, Dr. (Head of Retail Payments in the Division Payments and Settle-
    ment Systems, Deutsche Bundesbank)
Zetzsche, Dirk, Prof. Dr. (Université du Luxembourg, Heinrich-Heine-University
    Dusseldorf)

A.2 Questions from the Expert Interviews

Topic 1: Bank–FinTech Cooperations

1. Does the cooperation between banks and FinTechs generate lasting value? If
   yes, in what way and for whom: banks, FinTechs, the economy?
2. Should banks enlarge, maintain, or decrease the scope of their business
   models/areas of value creation? If enlarge or decrease, in what areas?
3. In what areas should FinTechs create value themselves and in what areas
   should they outsource activities?
4. Which general technological innovations (not business model innovations)
   have FinTechs developed?

Topic 2: FinTechs and Regulation

5. Should there be specific regulation that focuses on FinTechs?
6. Are FinTechs currently regulated differently from banks? Does that lead to a
   distortion of competition?

Topic 3: FinTechs and Privacy

7. Which privacy/data protection risks do FinTechs create?
8. How do FinTechs implement privacy/data protection measures (compliance department, chief digital officer)?
9. Do German banks have an advantage in customer trust over FinTechs regarding privacy/data protection?

Topic 4: FinTechs and Big Data

10. What are the use cases for big data in FinTech firms?
11. Do legal or economic limits exist for the use of big data within FinTechs? If yes, what are the limits?

Topic 5: Sustainability of FinTech Business Models

12. Do FinTechs rely on costumer data of banks to build a sustainable business model? If yes, which FinTechs and what costumer data?
13. How important is trust/distrust of customers in relation to established financial institutions when customers engage with FinTechs? For which types of financial services is this relevant?

Topic 6: FinTechs and Access to External Capital

14. Do (some) FinTechs actively target consumers or firms that have no access to external financing?

A.3 Terms and Conditions of German Robo Advisers

Company	Fees p.a. (%)	Minimum volume	Savings plan
Easyfolio	0.95–1.86	0 EUR	From 10 EUR
Fintego	0.45–0.95	2500 EUR	From 50 EUR
Ginmon	0.39	1000 EUR	From 50 EUR
Growney	0.39–0.99	0 EUR	From 0 EUR
Investify	1	5000 EUR	From 50 EUR
Liqid	0.5–0.9	100,000 EUR	No
Quirion	0.48–0.88	10,000 EUR	From 100 EUR
Scalable Capital	0.75	10,000 EUR	From 0 EUR
Sutor Bank	1–1.65	5000 EUR	From 100 EUR
United Signals	0.29–0.49	2000 EUR	From 0 EUR
Vaamo	0.49–0.79	10 EUR	From 10 EUR
Visualvest	0.6	500 EUR	From 25 EUR
Whitebox	0.35–0.95	5000 EUR	From 5 EUR
Wüstenrot	0.45–0.95	2500 EUR	From 50 EUR

Source: Websites of the companies, as of February 2018